Contents

ACKNOWLEDGEMENTS

The publishers gratefully acknowledge permission to reproduce the following copyright material:

© Anne English for 'Birds in the Garden' from *My Red Poetry Book* edited by Moira Andrew (Macmillan, 1988).

Introduction

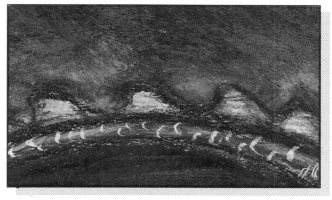

Scholastic Curriculum Bank is a series for all primary teachers, providing an essential planning tool for devising comprehensive schemes of work as well as an easily accessible and varied bank of practical, classroom-tested activities with photocopiable resources.

Designed to help planning for and implementation of progression, differentiation and assessment, *Scholastic Curriculum Bank* offers a structured range of stimulating activities with clearly stated learning objectives that reflect the programmes of study, and detailed lesson plans that allow busy teachers to put ideas into practice with the minimum amount of preparation time. The photocopiable sheets that accompany many of the activities provide ways of integrating purposeful application of knowledge and skills, differentiation, assessment and record-keeping.

Opportunities for formative assessment are highlighted within the activities where appropriate, while separate summative assessment activities give guidelines for analysis and subsequent action. Ways of using information technology for different purposes and in different contexts, as a tool for communicating and handling information and as a means of investigating, are integrated into the activities where appropriate, and more explicit guidance is provided at the end of the book.

The series covers all the primary curriculum subjects, with separate books for Key Stages 1 and 2 or Scottish Levels A–B and C–E. It can be used as a flexible resource with any scheme, to fulfil National Curriculum and Scottish 5–14 requirements and to provide children with a variety of different learning experiences that will lead to effective acquisition of skills and knowledge.

SPEAKING AND LISTENING

SCHOLASTIC CURRICULUM BANK ENGLISH

The *Scholastic Curriculum Bank English* books enable teachers to plan comprehensive and structured coverage of the primary English curriculum, and enable pupils to develop the required skills, knowledge and understanding through activities.

Each book contains one key stage. There are four books for Key Stage 1/Scottish levels A–B and four for Key Stage 2/Scottish levels C–E. These books reflect the English programme of study, so that there are titles on Reading, Writing, Speaking and listening and Spelling and phonics.

Bank of activities

This book provides a bank of activities which are designed to broaden children's experience of speaking and listening and enable them to develop their ability to listen effectively and to communicate clearly and accurately through speech.

Lesson plans

Detailed lesson plans, under clear headings, are given for each activity and provide material for immediate implementation in the classroom. The structure for each activity is as follows.

Activity title box

The information contained in the box at the beginning of each activity outlines the following key aspects:

▲ *Activity title and learning objective.* For each activity, a clearly stated learning objective is given in bold italics. These learning objectives break down aspects of the programmes of study for English into manageable, hierarchical teaching and learning chunks, and their purpose is to aid planning for progression. These objectives can easily be referenced to

the National Curriculum and Scottish 5–14 requirements by using the overview grids at the end of this chapter (pages 11 to 14).

▲ *Class organisation/Likely duration.* Icons ♰♰ and 🕑 signpost the suggested group sizes for each activity and the approximate amount of time required to complete it.

Previous skills/knowledge needed

Information is given here when it is necessary for the children to have acquired specific knowledge or skills prior to carrying out the activity.

Key background information

The information in this section outlines the areas of study covered by each activity and gives a general background to the particular topic or theme, outlining the basic skills that will be developed and the way in which the activity will address children's learning.

Preparation

Advice is given for those occasions when it is necessary for the teacher to prime the pupils for the activity or to prepare materials, or to set up a display or activity ahead of time.

Resources needed

All materials needed to carry out the activity are listed, so that the pupils or the teacher can gather them together easily before the beginning of the teaching session.

What to do

Easy-to-follow, step-by-step instructions are given for carrying out the activity, including (where appropriate) suggested questions for the teacher to ask pupils to help instigate discussion and stimulate investigation.

Suggestion(s) for extension/support

Ideas are given for ways of providing easy differentiation where activities lend themselves to this purpose. In all cases, suggestions are provided as to ways in which each activity can be modified for less able or extended for more able children.

Assessment opportunities

Where appropriate, opportunities for ongoing teacher assessment of the children's work during or after a specific activity are highlighted.

Opportunities for IT

Where opportunities for IT present themselves, these are briefly outlined with reference to particularly suitable types of program. The chart on page 159 presents specific areas of IT covered in the activities, together with more detailed support on how to apply particular types of program. Selected lesson plans serve as models for other activities by providing more comprehensive guidance on the application of IT, and these are indicated by the bold page numbers on the grid and the ⬦ icon at the start of an activity.

Display/performance ideas

Where they are relevant and innovative, display ideas are incorporated into activity plans and illustrated with examples. For many speaking and listening activities, performance is a more appropriate outcome than a display. In these cases, a range of performance activities is suggested.

Other aspects of the English PoS covered

Inevitably, as all areas of English are interrelated, activities will cover aspects of the programmes of study in other areas of the English curriculum. These links are highlighted under this heading.

Reference to photocopiable sheets

Where activities include photocopiable activity sheets, small reproductions of these are included in the lesson plans together with guidance notes for their use and, where appropriate, suggested answers.

Assessment

Assessment of speaking and listening is more subjective than that of reading or writing. Nevertheless, it is important to make a careful assessment and keep records of attainment. Each activity includes suggestions for formative assessment, and one activity in each chapter is designed for a more formal, summative assessment of progress. Photocopiable record sheets are provided for this purpose. These sheets can be used to decide on a 'best fit' level for overall attainment at KS2. Assessment activities and their associated photocopiables are indicated by the ⬦ icon.

Photocopiable activity sheets

Many of the activities are accompanied by photocopiable activity sheets. For some activities, the sheet is a resource which the teacher can use in various specific ways within the activity, in order to provide differentiation by task. Other sheets are used for recording, or for relatively open-ended tasks, in order to provide differentiation by outcome. The photocopiable activity sheets provide purposeful activities that are ideal for assessment and can be kept as records in pupils' portfolios of work.

Cross-curricular links

Cross-curricular links are identified on a simple grid which cross-references the particular areas of study in English to the programmes of study for other subjects in the curriculum, and where appropriate provides suggestions for activities (see page 160).

SPEAKING AND LISTENING

SPEAKING AND LISTENING

With the youngest children it is important to establish the habit of listening, not only to the teacher, but to other children in the group. Such courtesy should be encouraged from the first days at school.

A quiet area, preferably a carpeted corner, should be designated as a place where story-telling/reading is a routine activity. This will encourage the children to treat it as a place where listening is expected of them.

If space and resources permit, the quiet area should be surrounded with story books and picture books, all easily accessible to the children. Try to make the story corner an exciting place to be. Place story posters on the walls and have green plants, dried flowers and interesting objects, such as shells, fir cones or driftwood, arranged on the bookcases. As well as making the story corner more attractive, these artefacts can provide talking points for the children.

Early on, it is important to establish a speaking and listening routine for the children. They may need to learn the practice of taking turns to speak, and of listening actively to what others have to say. Teach the children the custom of putting a hand up to let the teachers know when they want to take part in the discussion.

Try also to make sure that everybody, even the quietest of children, is encouraged to take a turn – it's all too easy to be railroaded by the noisy, confident characters in the group.

Speaking skills

▲ *Confidence:* The children should be encouraged to talk to others and to listen to their own voices with increasing confidence; so it is helpful to start by asking questions which can be answered simply, perhaps by a single word – for example: *Where do you live?* As children develop, they can be encouraged to extend their answers into sentence form.

▲ *Clarity:* Children's speech needs to be clear, so that others can hear what is said with ease. Suggest games where children have to cover their eyes and/or listen to clues, such as *Hunt the Thimble.*

▲ *Coherence:* Some children who are just starting school may still be using a form of 'baby-talk', so it is important to encourage them to become more coherent in their speech. A few tactful questions can help to unravel what children really mean. This may require spending time with a small group. Often, as children acquire confidence, their clarity and fluency of speech improves at the same time.

▲ *Responding:* Learning to respond to what other children say is a higher-order skill of speaking and listening. To do this well, they must first have learned to listen effectively. Then they have to think about what has been said, before finally speaking or giving an opinion themselves. Too often, children rush into a discussion without taking time to think. Encourage them to respond positively and thoughtfully, so that they begin to learn the rules of social conversation. Their experience of adult behaviour may not always reinforce these rules; so it is important that their experience in school encourages them to have respect and consideration for others.

Listening skills

Listening cannot, of course, be separated from speaking. Children need to learn to take turns in discussion, listening carefully to the views of others and not just waiting impatiently for their turn to speak. They need to have an attention span appropriate to whatever activity they are to undertake. They should be able to listen with enjoyment to a story; to think about what they have heard, so that they are able to make sensible responses; and, most importantly, to remember what they have heard, so that (for example) they can carry out instructions or pass on information.

Overview grid

Learning objective	PoS/AO	Content	Type of activity	Page
Storytelling and performance				
To build confidence in oral participation.	1a, d; 2a, b; 3b. *Talking and listening in groups: Level A. Listening in order to respond: Level A.*	Performing and learning nursery rhymes.	Whole-class activity.	14
To develop attentive listening and response through repetition.	1a, c, d; 2a, b; 3b. *As above.*	Work on cumulative stories.	Whole-class activity.	16
Practice in oral participation.	1a, d; 2a, b. *As above.*	Inventing and performing finger plays.	Whole-class activity.	17
To develop attentive listening and performance skills.	1a, c, d; 2a, b. *As above.*	Listening to poetry and choral speaking.	Whole-class activity.	19
To develop attentive listening and response.	1a, b, c; 2a, b. *As above.*	Listening and responding to traditional stories.	Whole-class activity.	21
Extending vocabulary				
To encourage listening and use of alliteration.	1a, c, d; 2a, b; 3a, b. *Awareness of genre: Level A.*	Building alliterative poems.	Whole class.	24
Encouraging exploration of the vocabulary of contrast.	1a, c; 2a, b; 3b. *Talking about experiences, feelings and opinions: Level A.*	Brainstorming contrasting day and night words.	Whole class, followed by two groups.	25
Deepening and extending spoken language skills.	1a, c; 2a, b; 3a, b. *As above.*	Class discussion about experiences.	Whole-class discussion.	28
Encouraging the use of the language of classification.	1a, c; 2a, b; 3a, b. *Conveying information, instructions and directions: Level A.*	Classification work on food.	Class work, then pair work.	29
Exploring ideas and expressing them in everyday language.	1a, c; 2a, b; 3a, b. *Talking about experiences, feelings and opinions: Level A.*	Discussion and imaginative responses to the concept of time.	Class work, followed by group work.	31
To develop use of imaginative language.	1a, b, c; 2a, b; 3a, b. *Listening in order to respond: Level A.*	Brainstorming work on fruit, followed by storytelling.	Whole class, followed by individual work.	33
Extending vocabulary in unusual, imaginative ways.	1a, b, c, d; 2a, b; 3a. *Talking about experiences, feelings and opinions: Level A.*	Devising messages in bottles.	Whole class.	34
Encouraging the use of imaginative, descriptive language.	1a, c; 2a, b; 3a, b. *As above.*	Creating 'monsters'.	Whole class, followed by pair work.	36
Attentive listening to descriptive vocabulary.	1c; 2a, b; 3a, b. *Conveying information, instructions and directions: Level A.*	Building imaginary vocabulary on an animal topic.	Whole-class activity.	38
To encourage listening and vocabulary skills.	1a, c; 2a, b; 3a. *Listening in order to respond: Level A.*	Listening to everyday sounds and responding in an imaginative way.	Whole class.	40

SPEAKING AND
LISTENING

Learning objective	PoS/AO	Content	Type of activity	Page
Exploring the vocabulary of the senses.	1a, c; 2a, b; 3b. *Talking about experiences, feelings and opinions: Level A.*	Working on the five senses.	Whole class, followed by five small groups.	42
Giving children experience of using narrative language.	1a, b, c, d; 2a, b; 3a, b. *Audience awareness: Level A.*	Storytelling based on objects.	Whole class.	44
Practice in using imaginative language.	1a, c; 2a, b; 3b. *Talking about experiences, feelings and opinions: Level A.*	Brainstorming ideas about the sun.	Whole-class activity.	46
Building a 'senses' vocabulary.	1a, c; 2a, b; 3a, b. *Conveying information, instructions and directions: Level A.*	Looking at and talking about the weather.	Class or group activity.	47
To give practice in using the past tense and narrative language.	1a, b, c, d; 2a, b; 3a. *Talking about experiences, feelings and opinions: Level A.*	'Telephone' storytelling.	Whole class, followed by even-numbered groups.	49
Information handling				
To build confidence in speaking to an audience and responding to questions.	1a, b, d; 2a, b; 3a, b. *Audience awareness: Level A.*	Answering questions posed by the class.	An individual child talking to the whole class.	52
To give practice in auditory discrimination.	1a, b, c; 2a, b. *Listening in groups: Level A.*	An 'I Spy' game to reinforce key phonics.	Whole-class activity.	53
To encourage children to describe a process accurately.	1a, b, c; 2a, b; 3a, b. *Conveying information: Level A.*	Talking about growing seeds.	Groups of six to eight children.	54
To encourage children to go beyond one-word answers.	1a, c; 2a, b; 3a, b. *Talking in groups: Level A.*	Discussion of food likes and dislikes.	Whole class or groups.	55
To provide children with the opportunity to speak in front of a group.	1a, b, d; 2a, b; 3a, b. *As above.*	Taking on an imaginary persona by wearing a hat.	Group work, then storytelling to the class.	57
To enable children to use descriptive language with accuracy and attention to detail.	1a, b, c; 2a, b; 3a, b. *Talking about experiences: Level A.*	An outdoor activity, looking for secret places.	Small groups of four or five.	58
To encourage children to use accurate and vivid description.	1a, c; 2a, b; 3a, b. *Conveying information: Level A.*	Careful description of 'surprise' object.	Whole class.	60
To enable children to include relevant detail in description based on observation.	1a, b, c; 2a, b; 3a. *As above.*	Discussion based on teddy bears.	Whole class.	61
To enable children to describe a process, using the language of sequencing.	1a, b, c; 2a, b; 3a, b. *Talking about experiences and conveying information: Level A.*	Making and talking about 'junk monsters'.	Small-group work (making monsters), then presentation to the class.	63

SPEAKING AND LISTENING

Learning objective	PoS/AO	Content	Type of activity	Page
To give children an opportunity to converse confidently with an adult.	1a, b; 2a; 3a. *Talking in groups: Level A.*	Showing a visitor around the school.	Whole class initially, followed by pairs or small groups.	64
To give children the opportunity to organise and present factual information.	1a, c; 2a, b; 3a, b. *Conveying information: Level A.*	Talking about reflections in a mirror.	Whole-class or group activity.	66
To give children practice in listening to and repeating an unusual message.	1a, b, c, d; 2a, b; 3a, b. *Listening for information: Level A.*	A 'Chinese Whispers' game.	Small groups of six to eight, followed by whole-class activity.	67
Explaining and understanding				
To encourage children's use of descriptive language with reference to the sense of touch.	1a, b, c; 2a, b; 3a, b. *Talking about experiences: Level A.*	Feeling objects and talking about them.	Whole-class activity.	70
To enable children to listen to and pass on instructions accurately.	1a, c; 2a, b; 3a, b. *Listening for information and instructions: Level A.*	Learning a painting skill and passing it on to others.	Two groups of five or six children.	71
To enable children to explain how things work.	1a, b, c; 2a, b; 3a, b. *Talking about experiences: Level A.*	A science experiment, looking at burning candles.	Supervised groups of about eight to ten.	73
To enable children to explain a process in fluent, clear language.	1a, b, c; 2a, b; 3a, b. *Conveying information: Level A.*	Making a greetings card.	Groups of around six.	74
To give practice in making deductions through dialogue.	1a, b, c; 2a, b; 3a, b. *Talking about opinions: Level A.*	Talking and speculating about pictures.	Whole class, then pair work.	75
To develop children's use of descriptive language with reference to the sense of sound.	1a, b, c; 2a, b; 3a, b. *Listening in order to respond: Level A.*	Listening to and talking about sounds.	Whole class, then pair work.	77
To give practice in asking questions and thinking of logical answers.	1a, b, d; 2a, b; 3a, b. *Talking in groups: Level A.*	An imaginative question and answer game.	Whole class, then pair work.	78
To develop children's skills in accurate description.	1a, c, d; 2a, b; 3a, b. *Conveying instructions: Level A.*	A version of 'Blind Man's Buff'.	Groups for introduction, then paired activity.	80
To give children practice in explaining a familiar situation.	1a, b; 2a; 3a, b. *Conveying directions: Level A.*	Showing new children around the school.	Small groups of six to eight, then pairs.	81
Opinion and persuasion				
To enable children to use the language of persuasion and think of plausible arguments.	1a, b, c, d; 2a, b; 3a, b. *Talking about experiences and opinions: Level A.*	Improvised drama: persuading parents!	Whole class, then group work.	84
To enable children to put forward a point of view.	1a, b, c; 2a, b; 3a, b. *Talking about opinions: Level A.*	A class game based on three wishes.	Whole class, then work in three groups.	85

SPEAKING AND LISTENING

Learning objective	PoS/AO	Content	Type of activity	Page
To enable children to articulate a point of view and persuade others.	1a, b, c; 2a, b; 3a, b. *Talking about experiences and opinions: Level A.*	Imaginative work based on dragons.	Whole-class discussion, then work in four groups.	87
To enable children to express opinions about their feelings.	1a, b, c; 2a, b; 3a, b. *Talking about feelings and opinions: Level A.*	Looking at feelings by using colours.	Whole class.	89
To enable children to use the language of persuasion.	1a, b, c; 2a, b; 3a, b. *Conveying information: Level A.*	Talking about/ designing anti-litter posters.	Whole class, followed by three groups.	91
To enable children to put forward a point of view and argue its validity.	1a, b, c; 2a, b; 3a, b. *Talking about experiences and opinions: Level A.*	Talking about pets, and which ones are best.	Whole class, then small-group activity.	93
Understanding the effect of advertising; using persuasive language.	1a, b, c; 2a, b; 3a, b. *Talking about texts: Level A.*	Looking at and creating advertisements.	Whole-class introduction, pair work, then four groups.	95
To enable children to put forward a point of view in a group.	1a, b, c; 2a, b; 3a, b. *Talking about opinions: Level A.*	Forming and expressing opinions based on pictures.	Whole class.	97
Reasoning and speculating				
To enable children to make deductions and explain their reasons.	1a, c; 2a, b; 3b. *Talking in groups: Level A.*	A deduction game based on animals.	Whole class, followed by groups of five or six.	100
To encourage children to make clear choices and give reasons.	1a, b, c, d; 2a, b; 3b. *As above.*	An accumulating memory game.	Whole class, followed by four groups.	102
To encourage children to predict outcomes.	1a, b, c, d; 2a, b; 3b. *As above.*	Activities on thinking about unusual situations.	Whole class, then group work.	104
Enabling children to make simple deductions.	1a, c; 2a, b; 3b. *As above.*	Working on differences through class and group games.	Whole class, then groups of five or six.	106
Enabling children to speculate and discuss story outcomes.	1a, b, c; 2a, b; 3a, b. *As above.*	A storytelling activity based on pictures.	Whole class, followed by small-group work.	108
Enabling children to use predictive language.	1a, c; 2a, b; 3b. *As above.*	Imaginative speculation based on 'What if...?'	Whole-class activity.	110
To develop the use of elimination and prediction techniques.	1a, c; 2a, b; 3b. *As above.*	A class guessing game: what's in the parcel?	Whole-class activity.	113
Enabling children to make tentative deductions and evaluate them.	1a, c; 2a, b; 3b. *As above.*	A matching game based on occupations.	Whole class, followed by small groups.	115

Entries given in italics relate to the Scottish 5–14 Guidelines for English Language (Talking and Listening).

SPEAKING AND LISTENING

Storytelling and performance

All children enjoy storytelling sessions. When they sit together as part of a group, sharing the experience of listening to traditional stories and nursery rhymes, it is not only an important part of their educational process, but it encourages them to flex their imaginative 'muscles' and take a creative part in their own linguistic development.

Listening to stories is not the passive task it seems. Through these sessions, children can and should learn the skills of creative listening; making pictures in the imagination, thinking ahead to what might happen next, learning something of how other people behave and so on. In the safety of a group, they learn to share danger and disappointment, excitement and enchantment.

Nursery rhymes and traditional stories are part of our cultural inheritance and bring a love of language and listening to the children in our care. In this section, we suggest that children join in the rhymes and respond to the rhythms and cadences of poems, finger plays and stories by participating in repetitive choruses, looking for end-rhymes and taking part in improvised drama activities arising from the stories.

Such oral participation and active listening provide an enjoyable way into the vast traditional treasure chest of story and rhyme, myth and legend which is our national heritage. They also provide an important element in the development of early speaking and listening skills.

13

NURSERY RHYMES

To provide children with the opportunity to practise their listening and speaking skills by means of oral participation in a range of traditional nursery rhymes.

†† *Whole class.*

🕐 *10–20 minutes.*

Previous skills/knowledge needed

The children do not need any previous knowledge of traditional nursery rhymes; but to some, the rhymes will be 'old friends'. As this activity is an ongoing one, the children will gradually build up familiarity with the rhymes and may go on to choosing their own special favourites to listen to or join in with.

Key background information

The teacher should be acquainted with a wide range of traditional nursery rhymes so that she can lead the children into this activity. It is one to which she can return again and again – sometimes taking only a few minutes – so that the children begin to acquire 'an anthology of rhymes in their heads', until they become thoroughly familiar with the language and rhythms of nursery rhymes. Because the use of language in a nursery rhyme is already structured, this activity is an easy and enjoyable way for a class to tackle some of the early speaking and listening skills.

Resources needed

A selection of nursery rhyme books and posters, for example: *The Collins Book of Nursery Rhymes* illustrated by Jonathan Langley (1981 & 1990, Armada Picture Lions 1992) and many others, any of which would be suitable. One copy per child of the photocopiable activity sheet 119 and the photocopiable assessment sheet 118.

What to do

Gather the children in the story corner, making sure that everyone is comfortable and can see you, especially if you intend to use a picture book. Read two or three common nursery rhymes aloud and encourage the children to join in. This may be a new experience for some of the children who are starting school, but repetition will soon put them on the same footing as those who are already familiar with these nursery rhymes.

Encourage careful listening by leaving off the line endings occasionally and asking the children to fill them in. They enjoy doing this just as soon as they get to know the rhyme. You might start with:

Mary had a little lamb.
Its fleece was white as ...
And everywhere that Mary went
The lamb was sure to ...

The next stage is to leave off *lamb* and *went,* until finally most of the children are able to join in with the words of the entire rhyme. It is not a good idea to push 'learning by heart' at this stage, but it will happen gradually through repetition and enjoyment of familiar words and rhythms.

Use picture books and posters to enhance the oral and listening work. To focus the children's attention, ask questions about the picture. Look for characters in the background. Who might they be? What are they doing there? Build up an imaginary scenario for them. Talk about the clothes Mary is wearing. Ask the children to contrast them with the clothes the girls have on. Ask: *What do you think the teacher said when she saw Mary's lamb following her into the playground? Would she have to take it back home? Where could she keep a lamb until home-time? What do you think your teacher would say if you brought your hamster/kitten/budgie to school?*

Use the rhyme to develop children's language skills – for example, Mary's lamb was *'white as snow'*, but what else might we have said? *'white as milk'*, *'white as a cloud'*, *'white as a dove's feather'* and so on.

After working on the pictures and posters, repeat the poem again and get the children to join in. Show the children how to vary their delivery, following your gestures, for example:

Mary had a little lamb. (Quietly, hand raised.)

Its fleece was white as snow. (Getting louder, hand stretched forward and then moved sideways in jumps to suggest movement of lamb.)

Be sure to go over each new addition so that the children are able to add to their stock of known rhymes.

Give out copies of photocopiable sheet 118. The children can use this sheet for self-assessment in the course of the work. Give out copies of photocopiable sheet 119. Talk the children through the nursery rhyme, getting them to match words to pictures. In the last (empty) section, ask them to draw the picture to go with the last line. Ask them to tell you about their picture, so that you can assess whether or not they are familiar with the missing words.

Suggestion(s) for extension
Ask some children in the group to help make up a new nursery rhyme based on one they know well. Suggest that they look for 'matching' words (that is, ones that rhyme), for example:

Libby had a guinea-pig,
It was always in a hurry,
And everywhere that Libby went
The guinea-pig would scurry.

Harry had a wriggly worm,
It curled into a ball,
And everywhere that Harry went
The worm was sure to crawl.

Suggestion(s) for support
Help the children who are having difficulty with remembering how the rhyme goes by holding their hands and having them look at your face as you mouth the missing words. When they are more confident, let them work with a partner, at first putting in the missing line-ending, then tackling a whole line on their own, with the partner ready to help when needed.

Help children to develop new versions of rhymes. They could start with their own names, so at first it will be *Darren/Kylie/Inderjit had a little lamb*. Next ask the children to substitute a new animal. Help the children with the second line, choosing a word that has a number of rhymes. *'Sun'* for example, rhymes with *bun, fun, run, begun, ton, spun, gun* and so on.

Assessment opportunities
Look for the children who can/cannot find the correct left-off word in a known rhyme (see photocopiable sheet 118). Note those who can join in saying aloud a whole line in the appropriate place. Find out if each child can substitute his own name (or friend's name) to begin a new version of a known rhyme.

Linking the spoken word to 'marks on paper' (as in the 'Display ideas' suggested below) is a vitally important step towards the reading and writing tasks which follow in this Curriclum Bank.

Opportunities for IT
The children could use an art package to 'paint' a picture to go with the nursery rhyme they have made up. An adult or older child could use a word processor to scribe for the children as they make up their nursery rhyme.

Display ideas
Write out the new versions of nursery rhymes for the wall and ask the children to illustrate them. Next day, encourage them to read back the newly-invented rhymes.

Make a large floor book and copy out the newly-written rhymes. Ask the children to paint pictures to go with them, framing each illustration and pasting it onto the facing page.

Other aspects of the English PoS covered
Reading – 1a, c, d; 2c.
Writing – 1a.

Reference to photocopiable sheets
Photocopiable sheet 118 is a self-assessment sheet which the children can use to record their own level of success in the activity. Talk through the questions with the children, and help them (on an individual basis) to fill in the sheet. Photocopiable sheet 119 contains three pictures illustrating the first three lines of a nursery rhyme; the children have to display their memory and comprehension of the fourth line by illustrating it in the blank space.

SPEAKING AND
LISTENING

Performance ideas

Encourage the children to show their familiarity with old and new nursery rhymes by presenting them in class or school assemblies. Suggest that groups or individuals take a line at a time, sometimes repeating them making their voices very quiet, sometimes repeating the lines as loudly as they can. For example:

Humpty Dumpty sat on a wall (a soft quiet opening)
Humpty Dumpty had a great fall. (sadly)
All the King's horses and all the King's men (building up the volume, perhaps accompanied by bells and clappers)
Couldn't put Humpty together again! (voices falling to a whisper)

Performing in this way in front of a small audience helps to build up the children's confidence in being able to speak in front of others, and later to read aloud.

CUMULATIVE STORIES

To encourage children to listen attentively and respond to cumulative stories and develop their speaking skills by taking part in saying the repetitive words and phrases which are so much a part of this kind of story.

†† *Whole class.*
🕐 *10–20 minutes.*

Key background information

An understanding of the tradition behind cumulative stories, and of how choral repetition is used to build tension, will be useful here.

Preparation

A large card cut-out makes an excellent visual aid and can help to direct the children's attention to you, as reader or story-teller. First read the story through yourself and decide on an appropriate cut-out, for example, a turnip as shown in Figure 1 (or draw round a real one) for *The Tale of a Turnip,* a house for *The House that Jack Built,* a gingerbread person (or a real one) for *The Gingerbread Boy.*

Resources needed

A range of traditional stories with a repetitive build-up, for example, *The Tale of a Turnip, The House that Jack Built, The Gingerbread Boy.*

What to do

Gather the children in the story corner. Tell them that you and they are going to tell a story together, and that they must be ready to join in when their turn comes along.

If you are going to work on *The Tale of a Turnip,* for example, first show the cut-out turnip and discuss with the children what it is called, where it grows, what it might be used for. This kind of preparation whets the children's

Figure 1

appetite for the story and makes them keen and ready to listen.

Begin the story. *Once upon a time there was a farmer who grew the biggest turnip in the world. 'I'd like to eat that turnip,' said the farmer to his wife...* Choose a child to play the farmer and give him the cut-out turnip. *So he took hold of the top and...* Tell the children that this is their part of the story. To tell it properly, they must join in ... *he pulled and he pulled and he pulled, but the turnip stayed fast in the ground.* Get the 'farmer' to do the actions. (You might find that you have to practise the chorus with the children. If this is the case, once it seems that everyone is joining in, start the story at the beginning again.)

As the story progresses, choose a child to be the farmer's wife, the horse, the cow... (you can go round all the animals in the farmyard until the whole group has the opportunity to take part). Also include the tractor driver, the dairy-maid and so on. Each character in turn holds on to the previous one as they all join in with ...*and they pulled and they pulled and they pulled, but the turnip stayed fast in the ground.*

The last line is the cue for all the children to tumble on to the carpet. Finally, the farmer's child joins in and ... *the turnip came out of the ground with an enormous 'pop' – and they all had turnip for tea!*

Try to make sure that all the children join in the chorus lines and that everyone has a turn to take part as a character in the story.

Using the zigzag books, wall stories and floor books suggested in 'Display ideas' below, encourage the children to 'read' the stories to each other or to their parents. Ask the children to copy or overwrite the sections of text for the stories.

Suggestion(s) for extension

When the children have had further experience of traditional cumulative stories, suggest that they make up their own choral lines. They might experiment with the idea of an apple instead of a turnip. *...and they shook and they shook and they pulled, but still the apple stayed on the tree.* The family might be searching for a lost coin. *... they looked and they looked and they looked, but still the coin was nowhere to be found.* This work will help to develop and refine the children's listening and speaking skills.

Suggestion(s) for support

Help the children who are unsure of the choral lines by asking a confident child to start off and then getting them to take turns until the end, when they speak in chorus. *... so he pulled* says the first child, *and he pulled* says the second, less confident child, *and he pulled, but ...* (child one again) *... the turnip stayed fast in the ground!* (both children together).

Assessment opportunities

As the activity goes along look for those who are confident about taking part. Can they speak clearly? Are they ready to come in on cue with the choral lines? Do they listen carefully to the story sequence so that they know, for example, which animal/character comes next in the *Tale of a Turnip*?

Opportunities for IT

The children could use a concept keyboard overlay linked to a word processor to write the story, using minimal text. The overlay could contain pictures of the story which the children can sequence into the right order. When they press the appropriate picture, the related words will appear on the screen and can be printed out.

Display ideas

Help the children make the story into a large zigzag book or wall story. Use minimal text and collage-style pictures.

A cumulative story works as an excellent floor book. Use very large sheets of paper and have the children paint pictures from the story. Print out minimal text in large felt-tipped pen. Lay the pictures and text out in sequence and ask parents and their children to 'walk' the floor story. Encourage the children to retell the story to their parents.

Other aspects of the English PoS covered

Reading – 1a, c, d; 2c.
Writing – 1a, b; 2e.

Performance ideas

Cumulative stories offer many opportunities for performance. The dialogue is more or less ready-made and even the least confident children feel able to join in. Let the children mime the story, bit by bit, with the others joining in the choral lines as narrators.

If the story has to be performed semi-publicly (as in assembly) let the children wear a cap, a hat or a simple mask to indicate their characters. If they have made up new choral lines (see 'Extension ideas'), incorporate these into the action.

FINGER PLAYS

To provide children with the opportunity to practise their listening and speaking skills by means of oral participation in a range of new and traditional finger plays.

†† *Whole class.*

🕒 *10 minutes.*

Key background information

The teacher should try out as many simple finger plays as possible. The children will enjoy the activity of matching simple finger actions to the rhythms of the words. Often they are so busy watching their fingers that they are taking part in the oral exercise without realising it. This is an excellent activity for boosting the confidence of those children who are reluctant to speak aloud and can be repeated time and time again at an appropriate level.

Preparation

No special preparation needed, but a carpeted area is best so that the children can sit comfortably close to one another.

Resources needed

A range of song, rhyme and poetry books which include simple finger plays, for example: *One Blue Boat* by Linda Hammond (Viking, 1991 and Picture Puffins, 1992); *Round and Round the Garden* by Sarah Williams (OUP, 1983); *Twiddling your Thumbs* by Wendy Cope (Faber & Faber, 1988); *Of Frogs and Snails* by Yvonne Winer (Belair Publications, 1986).

SPEAKING AND
LISTENING

What to do

Sit the children in the story corner. Repeat the words of the finger play rhymes aloud, emphasising the rhythm. At the same time, use your hands to show the children how their fingers can be used to make shapes. For example, two familiar finger plays are shown in Figures 2a and 2b:

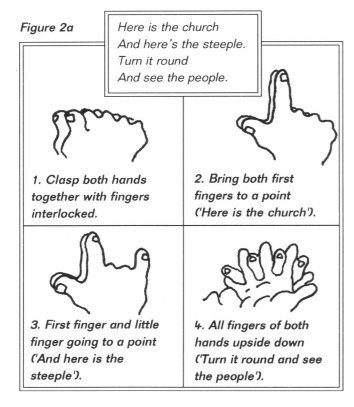

Figure 2a

> Here is the church
> And here's the steeple.
> Turn it round
> And see the people.

1. Clasp both hands together with fingers interlocked.

2. Bring both first fingers to a point ('Here is the church').

3. First finger and little finger going to a point ('And here is the steeple').

4. All fingers of both hands upside down ('Turn it round and see the people').

Figure 2b

> Round and round the garden,
> Like a teddy bear.
> One step, two step...
> Tickle under there!

1. 'Round and round the garden Like a teddy bear'

2. 'One step, two step...'

3. 'Tickle under there!'

Beginners sometimes find these finger plays hard to copy, but there is so much fun in trying that even very shy children are soon ready to join in. Take a few minutes a day to practise until the children feel at home with a range of finger plays. To test the children's listening skills, ask them to clap or touch the floor when they hear a rhyming (matching) word.

Get the children to make the church shape. Ask them to suggest what else this shape looks like: *a house, an animal with pointed ears, a tent, a mountain.* Ask them to make the 'people' shape. What else does this look like? *Flowers growing in the garden, people standing at the bus stop, trees in the forest?*

Talk with the children about some of the words in the rhyme. *Where would you find a steeple? Do you know what a steeplejack does?*

Figure 3

> Look at the flowers
> Growing in a row.
> Look at them swaying
> When the wind starts to blow!

1. 'Look at the flowers Growing in a row.'

2. 'Look at them swaying When the wind starts to blow.'

Talk with the children about different places of worship, for example: a mosque, a chapel, a synagogue.

Repeat each new finger rhyme with the children until they are completely familiar with the words and rhythms.

The children could make one big book (for group or class) or a number of individual books entitled *My hands.* On each page the children can copy the phrase *My hands can ...* They can draw pictures, overwriting or underwriting the adult words *clap, write a story, dress myself, make soap bubbles, help my mum,* and so on.

Suggestion(s) for extension

When the children have suggested different ideas for their finger shapes *(flowers, trees, a queue at the bus stop)*, use these ideas to make new finger rhymes. Figure 3 shows a possible example.

On a flip chart or whiteboard write a group poem, using the children's suggestions. For example:

Ten fingers to … wave goodbye,

Ten fingers to … do up buttons,

Five on the left hand, (hold up fingers of left hand)

Five on the right, (hold up fingers of right hand)

Ten little fingers

all out of sight. (Curl fingers up, hiding them away.)

Then put the children into pairs and ask them to invent and say aloud their own first two lines (one line per child), everyone joining in with the chorus.

Suggestion(s) for support

If children have difficulty in matching finger action to words, put them in pairs, one repeating the rhyme, the other making the finger shapes.

Assessment opportunities

Check that the children are remembering the words for themselves, not merely following the leaders.

Display ideas

Make a 'hand tree' by getting the children to draw round their hands, cut out the shape and colour it in, either in a single colour or by making a decorated all-over pattern. (See Figure 4.)

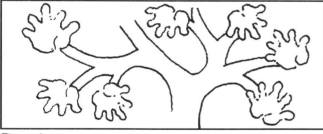

Figure 4

Make a set of hand prints by asking the children to dip their hands in paint (using various colours) and press them, overlapping, on to a plain background. This is a messy activity, but once it is finished, it makes a very attractive display panel. (See Figure 5.)

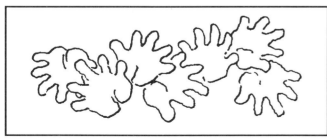

Figure 5

Other aspects of the English PoS covered

Reading – 1d; 2b.

Writing – 1a; 2e.

Performance ideas

Use a sheet with a lamp behind it and get the children to make a shadow theatre, one group saying their finger rhymes, those behind the sheet making the appropriate finger shapes. Some of the rhymes should be traditional, others will be those the children have made up for themselves. (See Extension and Display ideas.)

POEMS WITH A CHORUS

To provide children with the opportunity to listen attentively and with enjoyment to the rhythm and rhyme of a simple choral poem. To provide children with the opportunity to take part in a rhythmic choral poem.

†† *Whole class.*

🕐 *5–10 minutes.*

Preparation

The preparation depends on the content of the poem being introduced. For example, if you wish to begin with *Birds in the Garden* by Anne English (see page 20), it is a good idea to bring in a few peapods (if in season), a can of peas and a bag of frozen peas. Such props give the children a focus, but are not strictly necessary.

Resources needed

A selection of poetry anthologies compiled and written by contemporary poets. Use well-illustrated books intended for young children, such as: *A First Poetry Book, Another First Poetry Book, A Very First Poetry Book, Another Very First Poetry Book* all edited by John Foster (OUP, 1979, 1987, 1984, 1992); *The First Lick of the Lolly* edited by Moira Andrew (Nelson, 1986); *My Red Poetry Book, My Blue Poetry Book, My Violet Poetry Book* all edited by Moira Andrew (Macmillan, 1988); *One in a Million* edited by Moira Andrew (Viking, 1992); *Tiny Tim Verses for Children* by Helen Oxenbury and Jill Bennett (Heinemann (Mammoth), 1981).

Select a range of poems with a counting element or a chorus after each verse, for example: 'Birds in the Garden' by Anne English (see page 20); 'The Digging Song' by Wes Magee, from *A Very First Poetry Book*; 'Bananas and Cream' by David McCord, from *Another Very First Poetry Book*; 'Ten Red Geraniums' by Moira Andrew, from *One in a Million*; 'Five Little Monkeys walked along the Shore', Anon, from *Tiny Tim Verses for Children*.

What to do

This activity will use 'Birds in the Garden' as an example, but other poems with a chorus (that is, with a repetitive element) can be tackled in a similar way.

Sit the children in the book corner and tell them that you have a poem that tells a story. Say that one day Dad planted

SPEAKING AND LISTENING

pea seeds in the garden, but *someone* was watching! Ask the children if they know what kind of weather helps seeds to grow. Then read or tell the poem straight through.

Get the children to count down, using their fingers. When they come to *'One bird flew away'* let them flap their arms, finishing with a 'bird' on high flying down to *'gobble the lot!'* Practise the chorus once or twice, so that the children become really familiar with it and know when to use their fingers.

Show the children the pea-pods, the can and the bag of frozen peas. Ask them if they can say what is the same in all three and what makes them different. Once it is established that peas are the common link, pop the peapods to show the children the peas inside. This may be a new experience! Talk with the children about how the peas got from pods into the can and the bag.

Birds in the Garden

Four birds sat in a row
Waiting for the peas to grow.
One bird flew away,
Said he'd come back another day.

Three birds sat in a line
Waiting for the sun to shine.
One bird flew away,
Said he'd come back another day.

Two birds sat together
Waiting for the rainy weather.
One bird flew away,
Said he'd come back another day.

One bird sat on his own.
Rain came.
Sun hot.
Peas ripe,
He gobbled the lot!

Anne English
(from *My Red Poetry Book* edited by Moira Andrew, Macmillan, 1988)

Go back to the poem and encourage the children to take part in both the finger play and the counting.

Work on other poems with a repeated element in the same way, getting children to join in the repetition, so that they feel like storytellers. Find a discussion point (like looking at and talking about the peas) and then move back to the poem.

Suggestion(s) for extension

Use the original poem as a 'copycat' or template for variations. Perhaps you might think of four cats sitting in a row waiting for mice to emerge from their hole.

> *Four cats sat on a wall*
> *Waiting for the mice to crawl.*
> *One cat ran away,*
> *Said he'd come back another day.*

Suggestion(s) for support

Most children find it easy to join in this kind of choral poem, but where support is needed, sit the children opposite each other in pairs and let the more confident children lead. Suggest that the others are going to be like a mirror and copy what their partners are doing and saying.

Assessment opportunities

Once the children know the poem very well, say that you are going to make it into a game, pointing to someone to say the next line. It is thus easy to see those who are having difficulty in listening and/or speaking aloud.

Display ideas

To make a wall-display of the poem 'Birds in the Garden', cut out and pin up a wall-size fence. Get the children to make a huge pea-plant with a coiled stem in brown crêpe paper. (This can be stiffened with fine wire.) Ask them to cut out large green leaves in crêpe and make fat 'pea-pods' using painted papier mâché. Attach the leaves and pods to the stem. Using black crêpe and a black-painted body, make four large birds with feathered wings. (See Figure 6.) The children can make bright yellow beaks using sticky-backed

Figure 6   *Figure 7*

SPEAKING AND LISTENING

Figure 8

paper on pipe cleaners. (See Figure 7.) Figure 8 shows how the final collage wall-display might look.

Make a similar wall-display from other poems with a chorus.

Make a 'comic strip' wall book to illustrate each section of the poem. Print the words beneath each picture.

A reading and writing element could be incorporated into these displays.

Other aspects of the English PoS covered
Reading – 1d; 2b, c.
Writing – 1a.

Performance ideas
Encourage the children to act out the poem as a playlet or mime, wearing simple masks as appropriate. Put the class into groups and have them act as narrators, speaking the choral lines.

▶ TRADITIONAL STORIES

To encourage children to listen attentively and respond to traditional stories. To give the children a rich background in the language and patterns of traditional tales.

✝✝ *Whole class.*
🕐 *10–20 minutes.*

Previous skills/knowledge needed
Some knowledge of the convention of listening to stories being read or told is helpful, but not necessary.

Key background information
Many aspects of language pattern can be found in traditional tales. 'Magic' numbers, for instance, commonly feature – such as the three sisters in the story of *Cinderella*, the three bears in the story of Goldilocks, the Three Billy Goats Gruff – and provide a basis for repetition and refrain.

Preparation
Choose a traditional story to read to the children – ideally a fairly well-known one with which the children should become familiar, such as *The Three Bears, Little Red Riding Hood, Jack and the Beanstalk* or *Cinderella*. First read through the story and familiarise yourself with it. Decide whether you need props – for example, a glittering shoe for *Cinderella*, a velvet bag containing 'beans' for *Jack and the Beanstalk*, three different-sized bears/chairs for *The Three Bears*.

Resources needed
A variety of well-illustrated books of traditional stories from which to choose your reading. One copy per child of the photocopiable summative assessment sheet on page 120 (if required).

What to do
Gather the children together in the story corner. Make sure that everyone is comfortable and can see both your face and the picture book you intend to read from.

To make this a really satisfying listening experience for the children, first talk about the characters – what they wear, where they live, how they talk and so on. This helps to set the scene and frees the children to listen without the need for questions or clarification. Then read the story through once without additional comment. Encourage the children to join in with any repetitive words or phrases, so that they appreciate this aspect of pattern as a convention of structure and style.

When you finally close the book (or finish telling the story), leave a silent space before inviting comments or asking questions. This allows the children to mull over the story in

their imagination and gives them time to absorb it into their own experience.

Now ask relevant 'open' questions (those which cannot be answered with a simple 'yes' or 'no'). Take *The Three Bears,* for example:

▲ *Why did the three bears decide to go for a walk in the woods?*

▲ *Why do you think the little girl was called Goldilocks?*

▲ *Can you think of another name for her?* Blondie, Goldencurls, Susan. – *Why Susan?* Because it's a nice name.

▲ *Where was the bears' house?*

▲ *What did Father Bear say when he got home?*

▲ *How do you think Baby Bear felt when he saw his broken chair?*

▲ *What would you have done if you had wakened to find three bears looking down at you?*

Try to structure your questions so that the children not only have to remember the story *(Where was the bears' house?)* but are encouraged to think about what the characters say or feel *(How do you think Baby Bear felt? What do you think Mother Bear said when she saw her baby's empty porridge bowl?)* This kind of open questioning not only encourages attentive listening, but gives children some empathy with the characters in the story.

Encourage the children to retell the story in their own words. Write out a simple version of the text of the story, so that it can be copied or overwritten by even the youngest children. Let the children make the story into a large class book with pictures, comic-style. Put the book in the class library and encourage the children to 'read' it to one another.

When the children have heard a range of stories, they will begin to develop a feeling for the conventions and language in traditional tales. As the term goes on, introduce the children to all kinds of regional tales, such as 'Bhalloo and the Greedy Bear', 'Anansi at the Pool', and other stories from *Our Favourite Stories From Around the World* edited by Wendy Body (Longman, 1994); *The Wind, the Sun and the Boy* by Lynn Nixon (Bish Bash Books, 1995); *What Made Tiddalik Laugh* by Joanna Troughton (Puffin, 1977).

Suggestion(s) for extension

Ask a group of children to retell the story bit by bit, outlining where each child should start and finish. This means that each child has to listen attentively to the one before.

Suggestion(s) for support

For those children who find it difficult to sit and listen attentively to an entire story, offer a task such as turning the pages of the picture book or pointing out to the other children the relevant characters/colours/weather in the pictures as you come to them. Suggest that the children think of a question to ask at the end of the story.

If the children have made a large class book, zigzag book or wall story (see Display ideas), encourage them to work in pairs so that an articulate child can share the story with a less able companion.

Assessment opportunities

Attentive listening implies creative listening, so traditional stories offer many assessment opportunities. This activity can be used for summative assessment, and photocopiable sheet 120 is provided for this purpose.

Opportunities for IT

The children could use a word processor and work in pairs or with a scribe to retell sections of the story, which can be displayed alongside the pictures. The children should be encouraged to read their work (either on the screen or printed out) and then amend or edit their writing. They can select a suitable font and make it large enough to be read from a distance.

Display ideas

Have the children paint sections of the story. Frame each picture and pin them up in sequence. From the children's dictation, write out captions and place them beneath the pictures to make a wall story.

Let the children make zigzag books, drawing the pictures in story sequence. Display them alongside the original text.

Other aspects of the English PoS covered

Reading – 1a, c, d; 2c.

Performance ideas

There are many opportunities for performance, from a simple retelling of the story by one group to their classmates to a class play based on the story and performed in assembly.

Reference to photocopiable sheet

Photocopiable sheet 120 can be used for summative assessment of the children's storytelling and performance ability, based on this activity.

Storytelling and performance

Name: _____ Age: _____

Class: _____ Date of assessment: _____

Comments on ability in storytelling and performance:

Can talk to the teacher or other adult with confidence.	
Can speak with an awareness of Standard English.	
Can listen to a story with attention and understanding.	
Can take turns to speak and listen.	
Can recall details of a story he/she has heard	
Can think logically about the sequence of events.	
Can retell the story in her/his own words.	
Can join in the repetitive words or phrases of a traditional story.	

1 Working towards target. 2 Making good progress.
3 Has achieved target level.

General comments:

Extending vocabulary

Young children have an amazing number of words at their command, and their knowledge of vocabulary grows day by day. As teachers, it is our task to deepen and extend, in a structured way, their growing ability to use descriptive language.

This section describes a number of games and activities which give young children opportunities to use and extend their spoken descriptive language skills. They are encouraged to use words connected with their senses, to explore their feelings about the world around them, to speak in the language of narrative and of the imagination.

Good descriptive language presupposes active listening skills. It is important that the children are encouraged to concentrate on what others are saying so that they can, in turn, create pictures in their minds.

Our human communication skills are enhanced by increased knowledge of and interest in language. In offering the children a variety of speaking and listening opportunities which extend and deepen their ability to use words, we can help them to develop a lifelong love of language.

SPEAKING AND
LISTENING

ALICE HAD AN ANGRY ALLIGATOR

To help children to use alliteration and to encourage their listening skills.

✝✝ *Whole class.*

🕒 *20 minutes.*

Previous skills/knowledge needed

Some knowledge of 'key phonic' (the sound/letter with which a word begins) would be valuable, though not strictly necessary.

Key background information

This activity is based on phonic skills, but should be approached as a game, rather than as an exercise.

Preparation

If children are diffident about their phonic abilities, it would be useful to revise letter sounds. Make name badges for the children (sticky labels are quite adequate).

Resources needed

An illustrated wall alphabet, a range of alphabet books, flip chart, one copy of photocopiable sheet 121 per child, name badges, large cards inscribed with a capital and lower case letter for every letter of the alphabet.

What to do

Gather the children together in the story corner. Give out the name badges. Ask the children whose names begin with 'A' to stand. Go over the 'A' names: *Alison, Amrit, Anita*

and so on, emphasising the first 'a' sound. Suggest that this group sit together. Make groups of children whose names begin with the same letter. Give each group a large 'Aa', 'Bb' or whatever letter card to hold up. Use the alphabet books and wall chart to show the letter sequence in the alphabet.

Find out which group has the most children in it. Talk about how many are in each group, which groups have only one child. Again emphasise the sound of the first letters and ask the children to say them back. Ask all the children whose names begin with, for example, 'D' to stand, leaving a pause

for the children to anticipate what sound/letter you are going to use NEXT. Encourage careful listening.

Look through the set of letters which have no children's names. Ask the children to think of names to fit the sound. Using the names of children in the class, scribe on the flip chart one name for each letter of the alphabet, as far as possible. Encourage the children to read back the names.

Now get them to look for an animal, the beginning of whose name matches the children's names on the board. *Alice* can have *an alligator, an antelope* or *an anteater; Ben, a bear, a budgie* or *a bison.* Choose an appropriate creature and add the name or a drawing to the flip chart, so that it reads *Dines had a ... dinosaur. Maxine had a ... monkey,* and so on.

Keep as much of the activity oral as you can. The flip chart should be used to remind you what has been decided on for each letter. Now the fun begins for the children: they have to find an adjective to go with each letter. Suggest that (for instance) *Alice had an angry, angelic, amber antelope.* Help the children to look for words to say what kind of animal each child had. Do not take the first suggestion: encourage them towards a 'word-search', keeping in mind the listening aspect of the activity.

Should a child come up with an incorrect sound/letter, get her or him to listen very carefully. Emphasising the beginning sound will help those children who find it difficult. If *a giraffe* is suggested for *Johnny,* tell the children that it is the correct sound, but that its spelling is different – just as you may have a *Gemma* whose name begins with a *'j'* sound.

When the alphabet is completed down to *Zak had a zany zebra,* review the activity, getting the children to 'read back' the list. Encourage them to give it a tune or a rhythm, stressing certain words (for instance, the adjectives).

To finish off, give out the copies of photocopiable sheet 121. Ask the children to draw and name an appropriate animal in each box, so that they are consolidating their knowledge of 'key phonic' (that is, using an initial sound which is phonically correct). The more advanced children can add an adjective to match, for example: *a magic monkey, a maddening monkey.*

the children could also try this out to listen to their work read back to them. They may like to consider the difference between the computer voice and their own.

When the poem has been completed, they may be able to add an animal picture to go with their writing – either drawn using an art package or taken from a collection of clip art. Each child's page can be printed out and then bound as a class book or used in a display.

Display ideas
Make a large alphabet wall frieze with as many animals as the children can think of, painted, cut out and stuck collage-style beneath the appropriate letter. Put a collection of alphabet books on the display table.

This idea can also be used for a zigzag book.

Other aspects of the English PoS covered
Reading – 1c; 2b.
Writing – 1d.

Reference to photocopiable sheet
Photocopiable sheet 121 shows the letters of the alphabet (except for **q** and **x**), with spaces for children to draw animals (including minibeasts) whose names begin with the various letters.

Performance ideas
The children can work in groups to recite their alphabet list poems.

Suggestion(s) for extension
More able children can extend some of the lines in the alphabet poem. Tell them to look for something that the creatures did – for example, *Alice's angry alligator ambled along the avenue, Benjamin's bad bison bit his baby brother*, and so on. See how many of the lines they can develop in this way.

Suggestion(s) for support
Let the children use animal alphabet books to help them with initial letters/sounds. They should be paired with more confident children and should concentrate on the simple combination of a name and an animal – for example, *Freddie's frog* or *Harry's horse*.

Assessment opportunities
This activity provides a built-in opportunity to find out which children do/do not know the letters and letter sounds.

Opportunities for IT
The children could work individually or in pairs, using a word processor to write their own alliteration poem based on their name. They could start with their name on the first line, press the RETURN key a few times and then write the animal name. The adjectives can then be placed between the two. As new adjectives are thought of and added, the children can extend the length of the poem. They can read their poem aloud to each other, and may decide to change the order of the adjectives by retyping them or by moving the words using 'cut and paste'. If the word processor has a speech facility,

---

DAY AND NIGHT

To encourage the children to explore words and phrases of contrast.
†† *Whole class, followed by two groups.*
🕐 *20 minutes.*

Previous skills/knowledge needed
The children should have some knowledge of what is meant by *naming words*, *describing words* and *doing words*.

Key background information
The success of this activity depends on 'brainstorming' – that is, suggesting one connected word or phrase after another. Make this as quick-fire and exciting as possible, but indicate to the children that you expect them to remember and adhere to the rules of taking turns and good listening. The activity aims to build up a mini-thesaurus of contrasting words and phrases in the children's heads.

Preparation
Look out poems which describe night and morning – for example, 'I woke up this morning' by Karla Kuskin (in *A First*

Poetry Book ed. John Foster, OUP, 1979) and 'Counting sheep' by Wes Magee (in *The Witch's Brew*, CUP, 1989). Ask the children to bring in some of their teddies, rabbits, penguins and other cuddly bed toys.

Resources needed
One copy per child of photocopiable sheet 122, poems (as suggested above), flip chart, soft toys.

What to do
Ask the children to sit in the story corner with their teddies and soft toys. Take time to listen to the names and life stories of the toys. Encourage the children to talk about night-time, how the bedroom looks in the dark, why it sometimes seems a different place from daytime. Ask why they liked to have a toy to cuddle in bed with them when they were quite small. Ask if anyone still has a favourite furry toy.

Talk about night-time colours; *black, grey, purple, silver.* Talk about what they see when they wake up in the dark: *moonlight, stars, streetlamps, digital clock display.* (Be sensitive to any children whose home lives may have been problematic.) Ask if anyone has ever tiptoed downstairs alone in the dark. What was it like?

Give each child a copy of photocopiable sheet 122. Ask them to think about differences between daytime and night-time scenes. In the daytime: *sunshine, people up and doing things, a busy street , children running around* and so on. In the night-time: *stars shining, no people about (except for a policeman on the beat), cats.*

Now suggest that the children think about sounds they might hear in the day and in the night. Daytime: *children laughing, birds singing, cars zooming along, people talking* and so on. Night-time: *cats meowing, owls hooting, dogs barking, car alarms, babies crying* and so on.

Explore with the children words which describe the street by day and by night. They may suggest: *the busy street, the noisy street, the crowded street;* then, *the quiet street, the lonely street, the deserted street, the sleeping street.* Put one idea from each description on the flip chart as a heading.

Under the chosen daytime heading, scribe *In the day* and collect ideas about who and what are about in the street, for example, *little children.* Encourage the class to think about what the little children are doing and what sounds they are making, so the phrases become, for example: *little children running, little children falling over, little children walking with their dogs on a lead...* Encourage them to suggest ideas or embellish others' suggestions, working at a fast and furious pace. Tell them that this is called 'brainstorming'.

Use a similar technique to explore ideas for a night-time picture, scribing *At night* on the flip chart beneath the chosen night-time heading. Read the contrasting day and night poems.

Divide the children into two groups. Ask one group to find five or more things, animals or people (naming words) for the daytime picture. Ask them to think of five words to describe what the people/animals are doing, five sounds and five colour words. The other group should work in a similar way with the night-time picture.

When they have finished, bring the groups back together. On the flip chart scribe some of the children's own words and phrases to make simple list poems which can be transcribed as wall poems.

26

to draw and cut out figures and objects appropriate to a blue daytime frieze and a black night-time frieze. They should place the cut-out images randomly, one partly obscuring another, so that they have a patchwork quilt effect. (See illustration on left.)

Other aspects of the English PoS covered
Reading – 2a, b.
Writing – 2a, e.

Reference to photocopiable sheet
Photocopiable sheet 122 is a recording sheet on which children can draw contrasting daytime and night-time scenes, having first worked through their ideas verbally to establish relevant imagery and vocabulary. The completed pictures can be used to reinforce this language work.

Ask the children to draw contrasting scenes in the day and night sections on the photocopiable sheet, first talking with them about how contrasts can be built into their pictures (for example, by putting busy traffic, mothers with prams and children playing into the crowded daytime picture in contrast to an 'empty' night-time scene with cats, a solitary policeman, a car with headlights. Encourage the children to think about colour contrasts: blue skies and dark skies, sunshine and stars.

Suggestion(s) for extension
Take summer and winter pictures and ask the children to brainstorm contrasting words and phrases in the same way.

Suggestion(s) for support
Pair each child who needs support with a more articulate child. Encourage the latter child to suggest a simple naming word (from the photocopiable sheet), such as *cars.* They should lead the other child to find a matching word, *lorries.* Then a doing word, *cars racing,* followed by *lorries braking; Mums walking* followed by *children running* and so on. Let them create description bit by bit.

Assessment opportunities
Note which children are capable of finding five naming, describing and doing words relevant to the pictures. Those who have difficulty need support.

Display ideas
On a bright blue backing sheet, paste a round golden sun. On a black backing sheet, paste some silver stars. Divide the children into two groups. Give them coloured pencils, scrap paper, scissors and glue. Give one group the blue sunshine sheet, the other the black starry sheet. Ask them

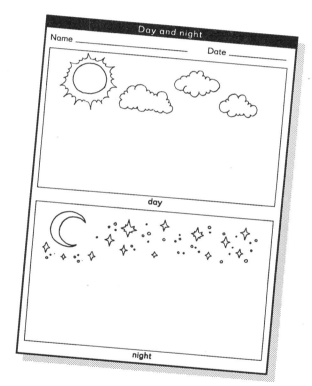

Performance ideas
Read or memorise the contrasting list poems. Then each child says a line at a time. One group can be dressed in sunny colours or wear paper sun-shaped hats. The other group, reading/performing the night-time poem, can either wear dark sombre colours or have silver star-pointed hats. (See illustration below.)

FIRST THINGS

To deepen and extend the range of the children's language skills.

†† *Whole class.*

🕐 *20 minutes.*

Previous skills/knowledge needed

Confidence in expressing ideas and talking about experiences.

Key background information

This activity is based on the idea of making lists – in this case, a list of 'first things'. Most children are only too ready to talk about their experience, but watch out for those who may feel uneasy about expressing their feelings in a class situation and be ready to boost their confidence through careful questioning and supportive comments.

Preparation

Find a copy of John Cotton's poem 'First Things', in *The First Lick of the Lolly* edited by Moira Andrew (Nelson, 1986). Bring in a photograph of your own first day at school, your first passport or something of this kind to help the children get started on the activity. Also look for a flower or a branch in bud – for example, a daffodil, a rose or a horse chestnut branch which is about to produce new leaves.

Resources needed

A 'first thing' of your own which you can share with the children, John Cotton's poem 'First things', a flip chart, a new (previously unopened) reading book or picture book, an apple, a knife and a plate, a flower or branch in bud (as suggested in 'Preparation').

What to do

Gather the children in the story corner. Read 'First things' and at the end ask the children if they can remember some of the things that John Cotton feels excited about: *looking at a new comic, going into the sea for the first time, the first day of the holidays* and so on. Tell the children that they are going to talk about all the best 'first things' that they know.

To start the session off, tell the children some special occasion you remember – perhaps, your first day at school, the first time you held your new baby, the first time you climbed a mountain or flew in a plane; or talk about something simple that you enjoy – wearing a new dress for the first time, opening a new book. Talk about the special feel of new things worn for the first time.

Ask the children to talk about their first day at nursery school. Encourage them to say how they felt (*lonely, excited, worried*), what sounds they heard (*children chattering, mum saying good-bye, the teacher telling a story*). Can they remember any of the people who were there, what they were wearing and so on? Encourage children to concentrate on their senses, what they heard and saw, how they felt. This gives a new dimension to the children's talk.

On the flip chart scribe *First things*, followed by *first day at school*.

Suggest that children think about the way the poet describes 'the first lick of the lolly'. Ask them about the anticipation of the first bites/tastes of foods they like; an ice-cream cornet, a freshly baked cake, a grilled sausage. Pass round the apple, asking the children to describe its smell, the feel of its skin and so on. Remind the children that nobody has ever seen inside this apple. When you cut it open it will be for the first time. (Build up the tension!) Then cut the apple into pieces, enough for all the children who want some to share. Can they describe that 'first bite of the apple'? Encourage the use of words such as *crunchy, tangy, tasty, sweet* and so on. (Add *the first bite* to the flip chart.)

Now produce the new book. Let the children hand it round. Ask them to talk about the special smell of the new book, the smooth feel of the cover. Encourage them to think about the story from the cover illustration. (Tell them that you will read the story later and add *opening a new book* to the flip chart list.)

Open the discussion to the children, asking them to talk about first things and occasions that were special to them – *seeing a new brother or sister for the first time, playing with a new toy for the first time, going to a new holiday place for the first time* – or the first swim/paddle of the summer, the

SPEAKING AND LISTENING

first hot day of summer, the first snow of winter. Add some of these first things to the flip chart.

Read back the list of 'first things' from the flip chart, giving it a sense of rhythm so that the children's ideas are gathered together to sound like a poem.

Finish the session by looking carefully at and talking about the flower or branch you have brought into school. Reinforce the idea of newness and new beginnings, that when this flower opens they will be the first people to see the shape and colour of the petals, to smell its fragrance. Leave a few moments of silence for the children to think about this.

Suggestion(s) for extension
Ask the children to think and talk about five 'first things' that nobody has yet mentioned. Suggest that they report back to you, using the language of their senses: what they saw, smelt, tasted, heard or felt when they encountered these 'first things'.

Suggestion(s) for support
Pair children, giving them a specific topic to discuss – for example, the first things they see and hear when they wake up in the morning, the first things they 'can't wait' to do when they go on holiday.

Assessment opportunities
Note which children are able to describe events fluently and hold their listeners' interest.

Opportunities for IT
The children could use a word processor to type and print one of their own 'first things'. These could be collected into a class book or used for a display. As each child will only type a single sentence and add their own name, the keyboarding time is kept to a minimum. If appropriate, the activity could be used as part of an assessment of children's IT skills (for example, using the keyboard, making capital letters and printing their work).

Display ideas
Cut out a large number 1 (to be used as a backing shape) for each child. Ask the children to colour or paint and cut out images of their own best 'first things'. Get them to glue these collage-fashion on the number 1 shapes. Pin the outline 1s at different overlapping angles on the wall and title the frieze *First things*.

Other aspects of the English PoS covered
Reading – 2a, e.

Performance ideas
The children can perform the list poem *First things* from the flip chart. It can be done as a round, with four groups starting the poem at different times.

LUNCH AT FIRST BITE

To encourage children to use the language of classification.

†† *Whole class, followed by work in pairs.*

🕐 *20 minutes.*

Previous skills/knowledge needed
Children need to be aware of the differences between certain categories of foods; for example, foods which need to be cooked and foods which can be eaten fresh. Many will use their own previous experience of watching parents preparing meals, others will need some background guidance on these differences.

Key background information
This activity benefits from children's experience of different foods, but it can also be quite simply based on their likes and dislikes. For those whose experience does not go much beyond ready-prepared foods, a visit to the school kitchen could be very useful.

Preparation
Arrange a visit to the school kitchen at a time when the cook has time to talk to the children. She might show them, for example, the contents of the store cupboard, the deep freeze – naming unfamiliar items. A visit to the fruit and vegetable department of the local supermarket could also be a very valuable introduction to this activity.

SPEAKING AND LISTENING

Resources needed

Pictures of staple foods, such as flour, sugar, milk, bread; some cooked foods, such as cakes, chips, fish in batter; empty cartons (for example, cornflake packets, frozen food packets); a selection of fresh fruit and vegetables (failing this, add fruit and vegetable pictures to the others); a flip chart or whiteboard; PE hoops.

What to do

Gather the children together in the story corner. Discuss with them their food likes and dislikes. Ask what school dinner menu, party food and/or picnic snacks they like best. Take a vote and scribe the result on the flip chart.

Tell the children that you are going to show them some things to eat. Use a PE hoop and place, for example, a green apple and a pear in the hoop. Encourage the children to make comments about them, for example: *I like apples more than pears. My mum makes apple pie for supper.* Now say that you have put the apple and the pear together because they make a set, that is, there is something the same about them. Ask the children if they can think of three things which make the apple and the pear a set, for example: they are both fruits; apples and pears both grow on trees; they both have green skins.

Take away the pear and replace it with a cabbage. What makes these things a set now? *They are both green. They both grow in the garden.* Lay out the pictures, cartons and packages on the floor. Ask a child to find something else to fit this set. *(Frozen peas, a picture of a leek.)*

Encourage the children to explore further examples of sets of food, for example, flour and sugar – you need both to bake a cake; a potato and a carrot – both are vegetables that grow under the earth. Get the children to talk about ways in which the various foods can be classified.

Divide the children into pairs. Give each pair a PE hoop and allow the children to choose pictures, packets, cartons, fruit and vegetables from your display. Give them five minutes to put things together to make sets.

Bring the children back together. Let them explain their reasons for making up each set. If they say simply that strawberries and cherries are both fruit, ask the children to put up their hands if they can suggest another classification. Encourage them to explore as many classifications as possible – for example, by adding a picture of beetroot to those of strawberries and cherries. What makes these foods similar? Can they find another one to add to the set?

Now suggest that the children help to make sets of food they like a lot/do not like at all. Scribe some of their ideas in list form on the flip chart. This list could be made into a list poem, to be read aloud and/or recited.

Suggestion(s) for extension

Ask the children to suggest other categories, for example: healthy food, party food, food that grows in the garden, food that needs to be cooked, food that is eaten hot, food that grows on trees.

Get them to make new food sets, letting the others try to guess what the common factor is in each set. Encourage a question and answer discussion.

Suggestion(s) for support

Get the less confident children to explore sets of colour: green foods, red foods and so on. Get them to make sets of vegetables, sweet foods, fruit and so on. Encourage them to talk about their choices.

Assessment opportunities

Look at the way in which children use words which show they understand comparative language; *the same/different shape or colour ... I like it more/less than ... it's better than/not so good as ...*

Opportunities for IT

The children could work in pairs to collect data about favourite foods in the class. Pairs could decide on certain foods such as types of fruit, vegetables or breakfast cereals. Once the children have collected the data, they could use a simple graphing package to display their work in pictograms or bar charts.

A more ambitious project would be to create a class database about different foods likes and dislikes. A simple set of data could be collected, such as:

Name	*David*
Sex	*boy*
Fruit	*orange*
Vegetable	*peas*
Drink	*milk*
Potato	*mashed*

Each child could type in her or his own information, so that a class datafile is created. Another adult would be useful here, to help show children how to do this. Once the database has been created, the children could use it to ask simple questions such as:
▲ *How many children like oranges best?*
▲ *Which is the most popular drink?*

Display ideas
The children can paint and cut out a variety of fruits, vegetables and canned food. Put the fruit in a cut-out basket, the vegetables in a box and the canned food on a supermarket shelf. Make a food frieze (or even a freezer food frieze).

Other aspects of the English PoS covered
Reading – 1b.

IN ONE MINUTE...

To enable children to explore, develop and clarify their ideas and express them in everyday language.
†† *Whole class, followed by groups of five or six.*
🕐 *20 minutes.*

Previous skills/knowledge needed
The children need to have an idea of time in relation to the kinds of things they do each day. They need to know that a second is shorter than a minute, and that a minute is shorter than an hour.

Key background information
This activity can be quite fast-moving and you will need to be ready with new and feasible ideas for what a child can be expected to do in a short span of time. Be aware of the aims of the activity – not just what a child can do, but how he or she clarifies ideas and goes about expressing them.

Preparation
Make (or acquire) a large card clock face with moveable hands. It is also a good idea to collect as many different kinds of clocks and watches (both analogue and digital) as you can. Lay out the clock collection on a low table.

Resources needed
A variety of clocks and watches as suggested above, a card clock with moveable hands, a stopwatch, an alarm clock, a flip chart.

What to do
Gather the children on the carpet. Make sure that everyone has a good view of the clock collection. Talk briefly about times of the day: when they get up, have breakfast, get ready for school and so on. Show these times, using the card clock with moveable hands.

Give the children the opportunity to comment on the clocks on display, if possible handling some of them as they do so. Discuss the differences in the clock faces (between traditional and digital clocks, for example). Talk about familiar and famous clocks, such as the town hall clock and Big Ben. Ask the children if they can say why clocks are important. Think about the morning alarm, the clock on the cooker, the school clock, the times shown on the video display.

Ask the children if they know why we rely on clocks so much in our everyday lives: getting up on time, getting to school on time, switching on our favourite television programme on time, etc. Ask them if they know any words to describe times: *second, minute, hour.*

Find out if the children have any idea of how long a second lasts. Let them watch the seconds passing on some of the watches. Now ask if anyone can think of something they can do in one second. Try out one or two ideas. *In one second I can blink my eyes. In one second I can clap my hands. In*

SPEAKING AND LISTENING

one second I can stand up or sit down. Encourage each child to think of a feasible idea, helping out if anyone gets stuck. Scribe *In one second I can...* and add some of the ideas on the flip chart. Add pin men drawings.

Show the stopwatch and demonstrate how it works. Ask whether the children can explain when and where it might be used. Ask whether they think that everyone can sit still and quiet for one minute. Tell them that you are going to measure one minute. Set the stopwatch and insist on absolute quiet, starting from... now! The children are likely to find it more difficult than it sounds.

Ask for ideas about what people can do in a minute. *In one minute I can walk to the door and back.* Now test this out with the stopwatch – the child can probably walk to the door, round the assembly hall and back in a minute. Take more of their ideas and test them until the children get a 'feel' for how long a minute lasts.

Let them divide into groups and ask them to think of three things that will take about a minute to do. When they have explored a number of ideas, they should discuss and develop them until they can decide on three real possibilities.

Bring the class back together. Each group should suggest their three best ideas, expressing what they thought as clearly and concisely as they can. Ask a child to try out one task with the stopwatch. If it is about right, the others can applaud the group for their idea.

Scribe the most successful ideas on the flip chart: *In one minute I can count up to 60. In one minute I can go to Mrs Thompson's door and back. In one minute I can say the alphabet four times.*

Just for fun, throw in a couple of zany ideas: *In one minute I could fly round the school roof. In one minute I could paint a rainbow across the sky.* Get some of the children to think

up more zany ideas. Add these to the flip chart – using quick sketches with pin men. Read it back as a *One minute* poem.

Suggestion(s) for extension
Ask the children to follow this pattern to produce ideas for *In five minutes I can ...* Give them the stopwatch to check out their ideas.

Suggestion(s) for support
The children could work in twos, thinking about what they can do in one second. Let them add their pin men sketches to a scribed 'poem' outline on the flip chart.

Assessment opportunities
Look for the children's ability to clarify and develop their original ideas. They should be able to show clarity of thought in expressing their ideas.

Opportunities for IT
Each child in the class could add their own 'one minute' idea to a class poem written using a word processor. The children could add pictures of clocks or watches, drawn using an art or drawing package or taken from clip art collections, to illustrate the poem.

Display ideas
Make two displays: a wall frieze with cut-out clocks and watches, and a table display of the clock collection. Add books and pictures and pin up the finished list poems.

Other aspects of the English PoS covered
Reading – 1d; 2a, b.
Writing – 1a, b.

SPEAKING AND LISTENING

 ## MAGIC FRUIT TREE

To enable the children to discuss a range of creative possibilities by using imaginative language.

†† *Whole class, followed by individual work.*

🕐 *20 minutes.*

Previous skills/knowledge needed

The children should be able to name some of our most familiar fruits: apples, pears, plums, oranges. They should also be able to recognise and name colours.

Key background information

This activity requires a leap of the imagination. Appeal to the children's originality, no idea being too unusual! (A bonus of this activity is that it may bring knowledge of what fruit looks and tastes like to children who are unfamiliar with it.)

Preparation

Let children name, see, handle and possibly taste some of the fruits which they will see on the shelves of every supermarket. If there is a cherry tree in the school garden, take the children out to observe it – best in spring, but the season does not really matter.

Resources needed

Fruits, as above – failing that, pictures or photographs of a variety of familiar fruit; photographs of fruit trees in blossom, and bearing fruit; a flip chart; scraps of coloured foil and decorated paper, glue sticks, safety scissors; a copy of the poem 'Strange Fruit' by Irene Rawnsley (in *Rainbow Year*, edited by Moira Andrew, Belair Publications, 1994); one copy per child of photocopiable sheet 123.

What to do

Gather the children in the story corner, making sure that everyone can see and hear. Show the children an apple. Let them handle it, smell it, feel the skin and turn it round. You might like to let them taste a small piece. Encourage the children to describe the apple through the senses.

Use the same process with a pear and/or an orange, lemon, plum. Now encourage comparison of the various fruits, concentrating on shape, smell and the colour and texture of the skin.

Show pictures or photographs of the fruit trees. Discuss with the children the kinds of fruit which grow on trees. Establish that they understand the sequence of leaves, blossom, fruit, seeds as the seasons pass. (This is not a universal pattern: the children may be familiar with trees which produce blossom before leaves, or seeds without fruit.)

Read Irene Rawnsley's poem 'Strange Fruit'. Tell the children that you are going to imagine a magic tree too, one which grows all different kinds of fruit at one time: oranges, plums, lemons, apples, cherries, pears and so on. Show

some silver and gold foil. Ask the children to think of colour and texture words: *shiny, starry, sparkling, glistening,* etc.

Holding a pear in one hand, an apple in the other, ask the children to think about a silver pear or a golden apple. Would the shiny colour change the taste? Can they imagine biting through a golden apple? Let them talk about this idea. Some children may suggest a distinction between *golden* meaning 'gold in colour' and *golden* meaning 'made of gold'.

Now encourage the children to invent and describe magic fruit for themselves. They might suggest *sky-blue apples, pink lemons, glass oranges* and so on. Can they move on to making up a story about a magic orchard, full of magic trees? Have they landed on a new planet? On a faraway island in the sun? Are they in a fairy tale? Scribe some of their ideas

as a narrative on the flip chart. Let the children read it back, adding new imaginative details as they go along.

Ask the children to describe 'magic fruit' using the language of colour and pattern, for example: *My magic pear is glittery. It has a spotty pattern like a ladybird's back.* Next, encourage them to glue coloured scraps of foil and sticky paper in an appropriate pattern on the pear shape on photocopiable sheet 123.

Suggestion(s) for extension

Ask the children to make up a story about magic fruit being delivered to the local supermarket. What would the customers say? How would the supermarket display the fruit? Imagine what the newspapers and television people would say. Help them to assemble the story, so that they can tell it to the rest of the class.

SPEAKING AND LISTENING

Suggestion(s) for support

Let the children discuss colours and shapes with an adult as they cut and stick their collages.

Assessment opportunities

Check to find out which children know the appropriate colours. Listen for their choice of words to describe shape and texture.

Opportunities for IT

The children could use an art package to draw a picture either of their own magic fruit or of an actual fruit. This is a good opportunity for children to experiment with different colours and tools (such as a spray) in order to reproduce the shades of colour found on real fruit. They may need to be shown how to mix their own colours, and how to select or change the type of spray to get the effects that they want.

Display ideas

Cut out a floor-to-ceiling tree shape in black card. Ask the children to make, paint, cut out and decorate collage-style a range of 'magic fruits'. Glue these all over the tree branches, so that the effect is one of brilliant colour and pattern.

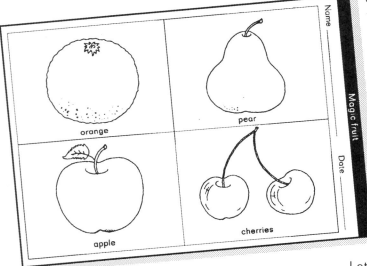

Other aspects of the English PoS covered

Reading – 2b.

Reference to photocopiable sheet

Having first described their magic fruit in terms of colour and pattern, the children have to recreate what they have described visually on their copies of page 123.

Performance ideas

Let the children make up an impromptu piece about visiting the magic orchard. Each child should take a huge cut-out of their own crazy fruit and use it in telling the audience about the new fruit: its taste, shape, colour and texture.

MESSAGE IN A BOTTLE

To stimulate the children's imagination by making them think of themselves in a new and unusual situation so that their everyday vocabulary is extended.

†† *Whole class.*

🕐 *20–25 minutes.*

Previous skills/knowledge needed

None, but any children who have been abroad on holiday should have a lot to contribute to the discussion.

Preparation

On sugar paper, prepare a simple treasure island outline, edged in blue (large enough for a child to stand on). Include cliffs, bays, sand, sea, a shipwreck, a treasure chest.

Resources needed

An empty bottle with a cork (if possible, use a bottle with an interesting shape), a bowl of water, pictures of pirates, a treasure chest (if available), the island chart, pencil crayons, one copy per child of photocopiable sheet 124, a flip chart or whiteboard, a picture story book about pirates or shipwreck (for example, the Longman Picture Classics version of *Robinson Crusoe,* 1995).

What to do

Gather the children together in the story corner. Talk about islands with them; what is special about an island? Concentrate their minds on the idea that an island is surrounded by sea. How then do we get on to an island? How do we get off? (By boat, plane, helicopter – it might even be possible to swim!)

Ask the children if anyone has been to an island (outside Britain) on holiday. Encourage them to tell what it was like, how they got there, if they could see the sea, where they stayed.

Lay the island outline on the floor. Look and talk about the various features: sea, cliffs, sand, rocks. Let the children add scenery, such as palm trees and mountains, in felt-tipped pen using ideas from the picture story books.

Tell the children that long ago, in the days of sailing ships, the ships were sometimes wrecked on rocks and the sailors had to swim ashore to fend for themselves on a far-off island. They had no mobile phones or radio with which to call for help, so they had to think of another way of letting people know where they were.

Show the children the empty bottle. Ask if they can work out how a bottle could help a stranded sailor. Experiment with the bottle in the bowl of water. Show that if it is corked, it will float. Encourage the children to come up with the idea of sending a message in the bottle.

Ask one of the more confident children to take the empty

bottle and stand 'alone on the island'. Get her to think about what message to send across the waves.

The message might go like this: *'HELP! I'm all alone. Please save me.'* The other children should ask questions of the shipwrecked sailor: *Can you swim? What can you eat? Where do you sleep?* Encourage them to think about the sunshine, the loneliness, the sound of wind in the trees and so on.

Give other members of the class a turn and encourage them to alter and extend their messages. This part of the activity should be completely oral – the child holding the bottle makes up the message. Ask them to consider the treasure chest: *What might be inside it? How could you use the riches? Would the gold and jewels help you to get off the island?* Each question should move the children's imagination forward, helping them to put themselves in a very exciting situation.

Put the word HELP! on the flip chart and give out the copies of photocopiable sheet 124, one to each child. Ask them to copy HELP! inside the bottle and to devise a message to add to this about their life on the island, either by using pictures or in writing.

Suggestion(s) for extension

Children could think of what would happen when the message was found. How might they try to rescue the sailor?

Suggestion(s) for support

Work on a one-to-one basis with children who need support. Use the picture books to help them find ideas.

Assessment opportunities

Listen for the children who can make the imaginative leap into an unknown situation. Make a note of those who are capable of expressing feelings, or of thinking of practical solutions to the imaginary problems presented by the shipwreck scenario.

Opportunities for IT

More able children might like to write their own messages using the word processor. You could set a word limit, perhaps 20 words, and the children could redraft their messages to reduce them to this length. They could be shown how to use a word count program.

Display ideas

Use the island outline as a backdrop and add children's paintings of ships, pirates and open treasure chests in a collage style. Put the frieze above a display table with an open treasure chest dripping with sparkling 'jewels' made from foil, old beads, coloured sweet wrappers and so on. Add some empty bottles bobbing across cut-out waves. (See illustration below.)

Other aspects of the English PoS covered
Reading – 2a.
Writing – 1a, b, c; 2a, e.

SPEAKING AND LISTENING

Reference to photocopiable sheet

It would be worthwhile discussing with the children the kind of 'telegraphic' (that is, minimal) language needed to fit inside a bottle shape. Encourage them to think through the kind of help they would need if they had been shipwrecked.

Performance ideas

The children can act out the roles of rescuer and rescued. Use a narrator to describe how the ship was wrecked. Stand a few children in a semicircle around the island outline, facing the sea, and have them repeat their messages asking for help (as though on a radio).

monsters with horns. Give one picture to each child. Photocopiable sheet 125 could be used for this purpose. Books featuring pictures of monsters, such as *Where the Wild Things Are* by Maurice Sendak (Armada Picture Lions, 1992), could be passed around the group.

Resources needed

Pictures (as above), a colour chart (a classroom chart with colour words or, better, a commercial paint chart), dragon and monster poems (for example, *Dragon Poems* by John Foster (OUP, 1991), a flip chart or whiteboard, copies of photocopiable sheet 125 (if required), various pictures cut from magazines (for use with photocopiable sheet).

What to do

Sit the children comfortably in the story corner. Read a selection of dragon/monster poems. Encourage the children to talk about what makes a monster – *It's a kind of animal, but it isn't real. It has a lot of hair. It's all different colours. It does some strange things which can be terrifying.*

Look at some of the pictures and ask the children to describe what they see, emphasising the colour and shape of the monsters and dragons. Introduce the colour chart, asking the children to say what the colours make them think of, for example: *Green like leaves on an apple tree.* They might use feelings: *red like when I'm angry, blue like when I'm sad.*

ONCE I MET A MONSTER

To encourage children to use imaginative descriptive language.

†† *Whole class, followed by pairs.*

🕐 *20 minutes.*

Previous skills/knowledge needed

Experience of looking at books and interpreting the pictures.

Key background information

This activity depends for its success on your ability to ask open questions which give the children an opportunity to exercise their imaginations. Try to move them on from one-word answers, for example: *What colour are the monster's wings, do you think? Blue. What kind of blue? Dark blue, like the bottom of the sea. Sparkling blue, like my baby sister's eyes when she is happy. Blue as the sky on a summer day... and so on.*

Preparation

Look for a number of different monster pictures – monsters with wings, monsters with big teeth, funny monsters,

SPEAKING AND LISTENING

Look again at the pictures and encourage the children to describe the monster picture using some of the colour language they have discovered from using the chart, saying perhaps: *It's got cherry-red feet like a giant chicken. It's got sharp teeth as yellow as bananas, as white as snowballs* and so on. Note, comment on and encourage vivid descriptive language.

Suggest that together you design your own classroom monster. Decide whether it is to be funny or sad, frightening or just silly, lazy or full of fun. Take as many different answers as you can.

Use the flip chart to draw the monster, starting from its head and working down. Its head might be *round as the sun, golden like a new pound coin.* Its body *as fat as Father Christmas, green as a hedge, spotty as a strawberry.* Try to keep up with the children's ideas, encouraging them to invent a really original, if outrageous design, for example: *with an orange helicopter on its head to help it fly, with a tail twisting like a multi-coloured rollercoaster.*

You may also wish to scribe the children's ideas to go along with the drawing, making up a list poem beginning: *Once I met a monster. Its head was as round as the sun and golden like a new pound coin.*

Ask the children to say what the parts of the monster on photocopiable sheet 125 look like and where they might have come from. Can they colour it in to show this? Ask the children to speculate about how they might design their own monster using cut-out magazine pictures. By cutting and gluing, get them to fill in the monster outline using, for example, a car tyre for the head, headlights for eyes and doors for wings. Encourage them to 'talk through' how to make their monsters from cut-up car adverts, kitchen adverts and so on.

Suggestion(s) for extension
Divide the children into pairs. Give one child a monster picture and ask him to describe it to the other as accurately as he can, with particular reference to colour and shape. From the oral description, the second child should draw and colour a picture of the monster. Having compared it with the original they can change places, using a different picture.

Suggestion(s) for support
Work with individual children. Let them colour the monster on photocopiable sheet 125, then describe the colours in the simplest possible way: *It's got red wings. It's got blue spikes on its back. It's got a bright golden tail* and so on.

Assessment opportunities
Listen for the children's descriptive powers: *as long as, as bright as, as spiky as... blue as the sea, red as strawberries, black as the night sky* and so on. Note which children can expand their descriptions by making interesting or unusual connections – for example, *with a neck as tall as a lighthouse.*

Opportunities for IT
The children could use an art package to create and print out their own monsters. Other children could use the word processor to write out their monster poems.

Figure 1

Display ideas
Make individual zigzag books (see Figure 1), beginning with *Once I met a monster.* The children can copy from the scribed work on the flip chart or write independently using their own descriptions. Each page in the zigzag should be used for a different part of the monster.

Make a monster world, each child painting and cutting out a different monster. Glue the monsters, overlapping, on a wall frieze. Use dark backing paper to make the bright monsters stand out.

Make masks of the monsters and glue them to plant sticks or old rulers. (See Figure 2.)

Other aspects of the English PoS covered
Reading – 1d.
Writing – 1c; 2b, e.

Figure 2

Here comes the monster

Name _____ Date _____

Reference to photocopiable sheet

The monster outline on photocopiable sheet 125 is used as a stimulus for discussion and speculation regarding its nature or origin and ways of modelling it.

Performance ideas

Using the painted masks, stage a monster march-past to music in the assembly hall. Read the class poem aloud (or put it to music as a song).

ONE BLUE BUTTERFLY

To help children to listen and to extend their descriptive vocabulary.

†† *Whole class.*

🕐 *15 minutes.*

Previous skills/knowledge needed

An ability to count backwards from ten. The children also need to have some experience of listening to and searching for 'key' phonic – that is, words beginning with the same sound, for example *bright blue butterflies*, *nine noisy nightingales*, *strong silent snakes*.

Key background information

This activity is based loosely on the Christmas song 'On the first day of Christmas'; so it would be helpful, but not absolutely necessary, if the children were familiar with the tune.

Preparation

Let the children hear the song 'On the first day of Christmas'.

Resources needed

A small jewelled or patterned box, a flip chart or whiteboard, one copy per child of photocopiable sheet 126.

What to do

Gather the children together in the story corner. Produce the box and ask if they can think of a tiny creature, small enough to live inside it. Go through the usual routine of 'hands up', so that everyone has a fair chance to make a suggestion.

On the flip chart, put the numbers 10 to 1 down the left-hand side. Now begin to write the children's ideas for tiny creatures, leaving a space for another word between the number and the name of the creature. It might begin to look like this: *10 ... ladybirds, 9 ... grasshoppers, 8 ... caterpillars* and so on. Do not fill in number 1 as yet. You might find it helpful to illustrate each creature as you go along – this will depend on the children's reading ability.

Now suggest that the children search for a *describing* word for each creature. Tell them that a describing word can tell how the creature looks or moves, or its colour or pattern. For example: *10 spotted ladybirds, 10 black and red ladybirds, 10 flying ladybirds*.

Explore the beginning sound of each creature: *ladybirds* begin with 'l', *grasshoppers* with 'g' and so on. To encourage the children to listen and use 'key' phonic, ask them to think

of describing words which begin with the same sound as the creatures themselves, for example: *10 lovely ladybirds, 10 little ladybirds, 10 lucky ladybirds*. Choose the most unusual idea or an idea suggested by a child who does not often contribute, and continue down the flip chart.

Encourage the children to 'read' the list together, emphasising the rhythm: *10 lucky ladybirds, 9 green grasshoppers, 8 curious caterpillars, 7 trendy tadpoles*. Give them the last two lines: *And one blue butterfly / swooping in the sun.*

SPEAKING AND LISTENING

Tell the children that they have made up a counting song – and they now only have to think about how to begin it. Perhaps like this: *On a cold Monday morning / inside a magic box / there were 10 lucky ladybirds / 9 silver snails / 8 wriggly worms …. until they get to And one blue butterfly / swooping in the sun.*

Now put the song to the tune of 'On the first day of Christmas' and sing it through with the children. Encourage them to memorise it. Give out copies of photocopiable sheet 126, and ask the children to record the song in pictorial form in the boxes on the sheet.

Suggestion(s) for extension

Using a similar pattern, make up a song about creatures in the sea, but add a movement dimension. For example: *On a sunny day at Blackpool / we looked far out to sea / There were 10 funny fish flying / 9 oily octopuses orienteering / 8 electric eels exercising / 7 jolly jellyfish jumping / 6 miserable mermaids meandering... And one red rowing boat / riding away across the waves.*

Suggestion(s) for support

For the children who find it too difficult to apply the rules of 'key' phonic, work with them one-to-one if possible, encouraging them to choose any suitable adjective, for example, *10 enormous slugs.*

Assessment opportunities

Listen for those children who struggle to find descriptive words, those whose language is limited to one or two possibilities, and the really articulate children who have a whole lexicon at their command.

Opportunities for IT

The children could use a word processor to write out their own or the class's counting song. To shorten the keyboarding time, each child could write out one line and print it for display in the classroom.

Other children could use an art package to draw pictures of the animals in the song. Once they have drawn one, they could be shown how to duplicate it to make the number needed. This can usually be done with a 'cut and paste' or 'duplicate' command. Children can then arrange the pictures on the screen before printing them out. Some software will allow the children to reduce the size of the first picture in order to get multiple copies onto a single page. An alternative but more costly way is simply to print out the number of pictures needed.

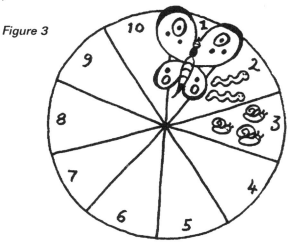

Figure 3

Display ideas

This activity can lead to some striking displays. One idea is to cut out a backing paper in the round, cutting it into ten segments. The title could follow the curved outline of the frieze. In each segment, let the children paint or colour and cut out ten, nine, eight, etc. creatures with the words scribed around an outside border. The final *And one blue butterfly / swooping in the sun* should dominate the rest, slightly overlapping the '10' and the '2' segments. (See Figure 3.)

Another idea for a display is to hang each individual 'verse' on its own illustrated rectangle, like clothes flapping on a line, beginning with 10 and going on down the line to 1. (See Figure 4.)

Figure 4

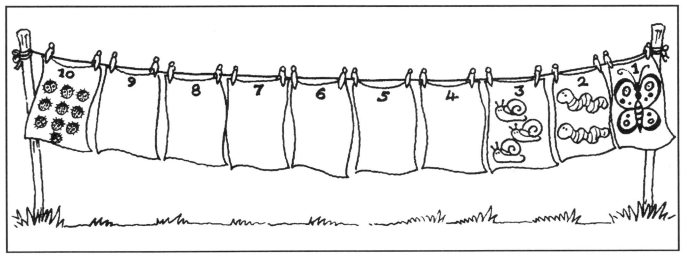

SPEAKING AND LISTENING

Other aspects of the English PoS covered

Reading – 1d; 2b.

Writing – 1c; 2d, e.

Reference to photocopiable sheet

Photocopiable sheet 126 is a recording sheet for use with the song. The children can draw pictures in the boxes to reinforce the song pattern. This tests their verbal recall and awareness of number as a physical reality.

Performance ideas

This is an ideal activity for performance, as it is a ready-made song. Let the children sing as groups, each taking up where the previous one left off. Finish as a chorus.

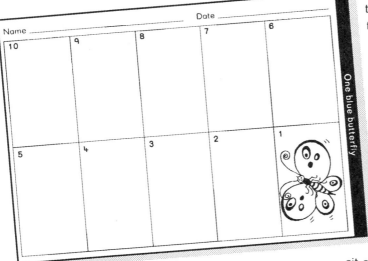

SOUNDS OF SILENCE

To encourage listening skills and to extend language and vocabulary skills.

†† *Whole class.*

🕐 *25 minutes.*

Previous skills/knowledge needed

The children should be able to use a tape recorder.

Key background information

This activity depends first on the children listening carefully, so make sure that they are comfortable, not close enough to interfere with others. Discourage whispering. The next part encourages the use of descriptive language. Give the children time to test and explore language by talking to each other. The two parts combined help the children towards discovery of the creative possibilities of silence.

Preparation

Prepare a tape with a selection of everyday sounds: a bouncing ball, a pencil being sharpened, a door closing, footsteps on a path, a toilet being flushed, a dripping tap, chalk on a blackboard.

Resources needed

A tape prepared as above, a flip chart or whiteboard, one copy per child of photocopiable sheet 127.

What to do

Gather the children in the story corner. Ask them to sit still, close their eyes and listen to the sounds going on

around them. When they hear an outdoor sound, ask them to put their hands up, but stay silent. After a moment or two, get them to open their eyes and ask them to tell about the sounds they heard. Encourage the children to extend their answers so that they begin to describe the sounds, for example, if they say *the wind*, ask what they could hear blowing, so that the answer becomes *the wind in the trees* or *the wind blowing papers across the playground.* You might want to go on to thinking about what the wind sounded like: *like a bird whistling, like a dragon puffing.*

Ask the children to close their eyes again, this time concentrating on sounds they hear from inside the school. As before, ask them to put their hands up, but say nothing until you are ready. Then ask the children who they heard, *the dinner ladies ... what do you think they are doing? putting out tables for lunch ... how do you think they are feeling? happy because we could hear them laughing.* Get them to put the ideas together so that their answer becomes something like: *We heard the dinner ladies laughing as they were putting out the tables for lunch. They sounded happy.*

Tell the children that they are going to listen to a sound on tape and that they are to guess what is making it. (Again, hands up, say nothing until you are ready.) Play one sound. Ask whether it is an outdoor or an indoor sound. *Indoor. What is making the sound?* (You might not get the correct answer first time round. Let them consider and speculate.) *It's a pencil being sharpened.*

When you have worked through the sounds on tape, ask the children to listen to silence. What makes silence? *No sound at all. Nothing moving. Quietness* and so on. When no-one in the classroom speaks or moves, is it silent? What sounds can they still hear? Do those sounds come from within the school, or from outside?

Now get the children to think of creatures that apparently make no sound at all. *Butterflies, ants, goldfish, ladybirds* and so on. (If they suggest a mouse, explain that it is quite a noisy creature: it makes scratching and gnawing sounds, and pitter-patters around.) Now encourage the children to think of what these 'silent' creatures are doing, starting with the phrase: *'Silence is' a butterfly stepping on a flower, a goldfish swimming in the pond, a ladybird climbing a stem* and so on.

Go on to think about things that they can do which do not make a noise: *thinking about things, my fingernails growing, my eyes opening* and so on.

Use the flip chart to scribe ten *'Silence is'* ideas as a list: Silence is:

▲ *my hair growing*

▲ *a dragonfly hovering over the pond*

▲ *me making up a poem in my head.*

Encourage the children to be as creative in their ideas as possible, always keeping in mind the need to extend vocabulary skills.

Get the children to copy selectively from the flip chart on to photocopiable sheet 127, making the list into a poem.

Suggestion(s) for extension

Ask a group of confident children to look for six 'silent sounds' of the school day, six 'silent sounds' from the school garden, six 'silent things' about their own homes and so on. They can go on to draw, or write and draw, their 'sounds of silence' in list form.

Suggestion(s) for support

Use the tape, one sound at a time, asking an adult to work in a one-to-one situation with the children who need help to listen carefully. Get them to help the children to describe what is happening on the tape.

Assessment opportunities

Use this activity to test the children's listening skills. Note those who can/cannot listen to the sounds around them.

41

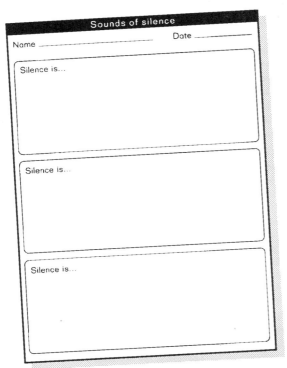

Sounds of silence

Name _____ Date _____

Silence is...

Silence is...

Silence is...

Can they distinguish indoor from outdoor sounds? Listen for the creative use of descriptive language. Note those who contribute imaginative ideas for the 'sounds of silence'.

Opportunities for IT

If children are given opportunities to use the tape recorder, pressing the various buttons to control the position of the tape, this will contribute to their experiences of controlling everyday devices.

The children could use a word processor either to write and print their own 'silence' poems or to write out the flip chart list.

Display ideas

Have the children copy the entire flip chart list as a *Sounds of silence* poem. Decorate it with a border of silent creatures: butterflies, ladybirds, snails and caterpillars.

Make *Sounds of Silence* floor books, illustrated by the children.

Other aspects of the English PoS covered

Reading – 1d.
Writing – 2a, b, e.

Reference to photocopiable sheet

Fill in the sheet to make a *Silence is* list poem, using drawing or copying from the flip chart.

Performance ideas

The children can perform their *Sounds of silence* poems to others in the school, perhaps as an assembly item where the topic is *The senses* or *Our wonderful world.*

THE SENSES

To help children explore the vocabulary of the senses in order to develop their ability to express their perceptions of themselves and the world around them.
†† *Whole class, then five small groups.*
🕐 *20 minutes.*

Previous skills/knowledge needed

The children should have previous experience of sharing ideas and feel at ease with taking part in a class discussion.

Key background information

This activity provides the children not only with the opportunity to extend and deepen their knowledge of language, but also with a considerable degree of excitement, so it is important to stress the rules of listening and taking turns to talk.

Preparation

Try to provide two natural materials for each sense. These should give contrasting sensory experiences, so that the children have a variety of interesting words and descriptions to choose from. For example: *touch*, a smooth shell and a rough stone, or a smooth pebble and a rough-surfaced shell; *smell*, a sweet-smelling flower and an orange or an onion; *taste*, a lemon and some sugar; *sound*, bells and a drum; *sight,* two contrasting pictures or photographs.

Resources needed

Two contrasting sense materials for each group (as suggested above), one copy per child of photocopiable sheet 128, coloured pencils, a flip chart.

What to do

Gather the class together in the story corner. Ask each child to look at the person nearest to him or her so that they can tell you the colour of her or his eyes or something about her or his hair. When they have responded, ask them to look (for example) out of the window, at the back wall of the classroom, on the top of the cupboard and say what they can see there.

When they have responded, talk about how we use our eyes. Ask the children if they can think of another word for seeing: *looking, staring, vision, sight.*

Get the children to close their eyes. Tap on the desk with your fingers, close a book with a snap, whistle or sing. When the children have opened their eyes, get them to talk about what they have heard and how they knew what you were doing without looking. Suggest that they close their eyes again and listen to the sounds from outside and inside the school. Establish the idea of listening and look for more connected words, for example: *hearing, ears, sounds.*

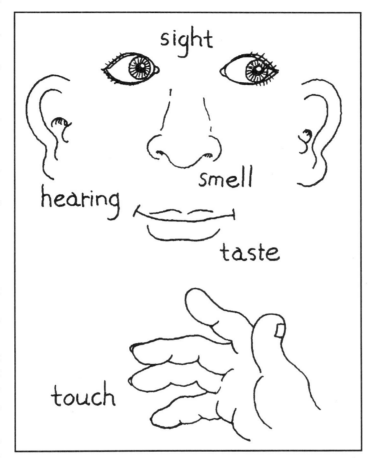

Now ask the children to touch things around them, the carpet, a neighbour's jumper, their own hair, the skin on their face and so on. Establish the idea of touch and suggest that the children look for words to describe how, for example, the carpet feels: *hairy, rough, woolly* and so on. Look for more contrasting touch words.

On the flip chart draw eyes, ears, a nose, a mouth and a hand. Establish with the children what senses we use ears and eyes, hands, noses and mouths for. Reinforce the sensory words we use: *touch (feeling), sight (looking), sounds (hearing), taste, smell.*

Tell the children that you are going to make a group for each of the five senses and that they are to touch, look at, smell, taste or listen to two things. They should try to find lots of sensory words to describe each thing – just as (for

instance) they thought of lots of words to describe the feel of the carpet.

Put the children into the groups and give out the contrasting materials to each. Give them five minutes to think about the descriptions before they report back. (This part of the activity generates a lot of noise!)

When the five minutes are up, get the class back together. Ask the 'touch' group to say what they found: *A rough stone, heavy, scratchy* (like what?) *like my grandad's chin, bumpy* (like what?) *like a cattle grid.* Pass the stone round and collect more ideas from the others, always keeping the idea of expanding and exploring their language skills. Go on to do this with the other four groups.

Scribe some of the new words and phrases on the flip chart beside the appropriate drawing. Give out the copies of photocopiable sheet 128. Help the children to read the words printed in the boxes. Ask them to give ideas (from their previous experience with natural materials) of things which will be suitable to go into each box, for example: *orange, onion, sugar* for the taste box. Ask the children to draw and label two appropriate items for each marked box. Encourage them to express ideas about 'our wonderful world' to make a picture for the blank box; this could be the world as seen from space, or a beautiful natural scene.

Bring the session to a close by talking about our five senses and how we use them to find out about the world.

Suggestion(s) for extension

The groups should be kept small (no more than six or so, preferably working with an adult). The children can extend their imagery by thinking, perhaps, of the feel of darkness, the colour of the wind, the sound of bluebells, the taste of holidays and so on. Scribe their best ideas into a *Senses* list poem.

Suggestion(s) for support

Explore one sense at a time simply looking for contrasting words: *rough/smooth, heavy/light, shiny/dull* and so on.

Assessment opportunities

This activity offers boundless opportunities for assessment. Can the children use contrasting words and phrases? Can they find more than one description for everything? Can they move on to the more demanding language and imagery demanded in the Extension suggestion above?

Display ideas

Make a large five-panelled frieze with collage-type pictures of things we see, hear, touch, smell and taste. Print the title, *Our five senses,* on a half-moon shape placed above. On the display table, in front of open books about the senses (sight), put a basket of fruit (taste), a vase of flowers and bottles of perfume (smell), percussion instruments (sound), and stones and shells (touch).

Other aspects of the English PoS covered

Reading – 2c.
Writing – 1b, c; 2b, e.

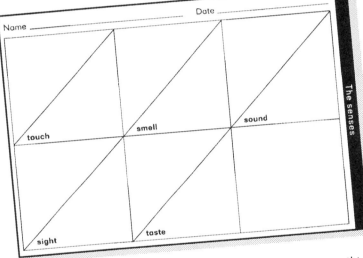

Reference to photocopiable sheet

Photocopiable sheet 128 is a stimulus for the children to draw appropriate images for each of the five senses, after discussion.

Performance ideas

Let children from each of the five groups make up a presentation piece which illustrates the sense they have worked on and which uses some of the descriptive words and phrases they have found. For example: *I have eyes and I can see the dark sky at night. I have eyes and I can see silver stars lighting up the dark. But* (in contrast) *I have eyes and I can see the golden sun of morning. I have eyes and I can see the bright blue sky of summer.* The sound group could present the following: *I have ears and I can hear the deep thunder of the drums...* This goes well against a percussion background.

THE STORY BOX

To give children experience of using narrative language.
†† *Whole class.*
🕐 *25 minutes.*

Previous skills/knowledge needed

The children should be used to listening to a variety of story forms.

Key background information

This activity depends on an element of surprise. The story box itself provides its own interest, each successive element taking the story a step further. Your task is to exploit the imaginative possibilities which children will bring to building up a satisfactory narrative.

Preparation

Gather together a set of models to provide the elements of the story, for example: something like a bee or a butterfly, a cat or a cockerel as the main character; a plastic flower or bunch of holly; a 'gem', a black plastic spider or a sparkling ring; a model church, castle, toadstool or cottage. These artefacts answer the narrative questions: *Who is the story about? Where was he/she? What did he/she find? What happened?* Hide the story elements in a decorated box.

Resources needed

Elements of the story (as above), a decorated box, a flip chart.

What to do

Gather the children in the story corner. Ask them to think about where stories come from: books, cassettes, television and so on. Guide them towards the idea that someone somewhere has told, thought about, imagined or written the stories we read in books.

With an air of mystery, show the children the 'story box'. Tell them that there is a story hidden inside and the only way of telling it is for them to make it up. Suggest that the story will not arrive all at once, but that it will grow bit by bit.

Open the lid a little way and take out the first character: the butterfly, china cat or whatever. Encourage the children to look carefully at the butterfly's wings, at the cat's shiny black coat. Imagine the butterfly (or the cat) waking on a fine sunny morning. Imagine it stretching, polishing its wings or washing its fur and whiskers.

Encourage the children to think of a name for the main character: Betsy Butterfly, Benjamin Butterfly, Charlie Cat and so on. When they have decided on a name, it is time to begin the story. Tell them that Betsy Butterfly wanted to go on an adventure. Help the children to find a good beginning

SPEAKING AND LISTENING

for their story. *'Once upon a time Betsy Butterfly woke up early. She could feel the warm sunshine on her wings. She wanted to go on an adventure, so this is what she said ...'*

Get the children to imagine what she said, for example: *'It's a lovely day and I'm bored.' 'I wish I didn't have to go to school on a sunny day like this.' 'I'm feeling very brave, so I'm going on a brave adventure.'*

Use the flip chart to make notes on how the story is going. Then take the second part of the narrative out of the box; the flower or the holly. Help the children to weave the next part of the story, answering *'Where did she go?'* like this, perhaps: *Betsy flew off to a beautiful garden. There she saw a bright yellow rose, shining like the sun. 'I'll rest here,' she thought.*

Betsy looked down. There she found, hiding in the grass, a sparkling ring (or a big black spider). Get the children to think about what she found, how it might have been lost and so on. Now, the last part of the story, *What happened to Betsy?* Produce the castle, toadstool, cottage and ask the children for ideas about who lives there, what happened to the ring (or the spider) and, of course, how the story ends.

Betsy flew to the castle where a giant lived. 'Give me that ring!' he shouted. 'It belongs to the Queen!' Or it might be the spider's grandmother's cottage. Or a magic toadstool. Help the children to find a satisfactory ending in which the butterfly reaches home safely – with or without a reward!

Scribe the story on the flip chart in four sections. Get the children to 'read' it back, putting in description and dialogue

where they feel it sounds best. Encourage them to use narrative phrases, such as *'Then...' 'Next...' 'Afterwards...' 'At last...'* to make the story flow towards its satisfactory ending.

Suggestion(s) for extension

Provide a group (or groups) with different sets of story elements (and narrative structures, perhaps) and suggest that they make up stories which they can retell to the others.

Suggestion(s) for support

With children who are less confident, work with them in small groups, asking each to tell you one thing about the main character; name, description, where he wanted to go. Build up a simple narrative from these ideas, leaving out the dialogue if necessary.

Assessment opportunities

Listen for the use of linking narrative phrases.

Opportunities for IT

The children could use a word processor to write the story beneath the pictures used for the class display.

Display ideas

Divide the children into groups (of about four), each group painting a collage of a different part of the story. Make sure that they all have backgrounds of equal size, then put the story together as a wall strip cartoon. Scribe the story beneath the pictures. (See Figure 5.)

Figure 5

Other aspects of the English PoS covered

Reading – 1c; 2c; 3.
Writing – 1a, c; 2a, b.

Performance ideas

Some of the children can be encouraged to 'act out' their stories before an audience. They may enjoy using minimal props, for example, a sprig of holly, a marigold or a painted and cut-out flower. The author of each story can act as narrator.

THE SUN

To give the children practice in using imaginative language.

†† *Whole class.*

🕐 *20 minutes.*

⚠ *Warn children not to look directly at the sun.*

Previous skills/knowledge needed
Confidence in expressing ideas aloud.

Key background information
This activity leads to children thinking in 'images', the building blocks of poetry. This is a useful technique both at this oral level and later, when children are ready to express their ideas in writing.

Resources needed
Pictures or photographs of the sun, plus illustrations of children playing outside on a sunny day; a flip chart; pencil crayons; an orange, a yellow ball or a yellow balloon; one copy per child of photocopiable sheet 129.

What to do
This activity gets off to a flying start on a gloriously sunny day, but don't worry too much about the weather – pictures or photographs can also work well. Gather the children together in the story corner or, even better, outside on the grass in the shade of a tree, making sure that they do not look directly into the sun.

Suggest that the children are going to 'think like poets'. Tell them that poets are good at making pictures in their heads. Remind them that we can all do this when we are listening to a story or a poem being read aloud. Talk about using *imagination* – another way of saying 'making pictures in our heads'.

Ask the children to show the shape of the sun, by 'drawing in the air'. Establish that it is round – round like a ....? Encourage the children to give a variety of answers: *round like a ball, round like a penny, round like a pizza...* and so on.

Show the children the ball or blown-up balloon. Ask if they can say why we might think it is a bit like the sun. What things are the same? *It's yellow like the sun. It's round like the sun. It floats in the sky like the sun...* and so on. Take as many ideas as the children can come up with. Ask them to think of other toys that are like the sun; *a yellow frisbee, a football, a beach ball, a hoop, a bouncy ball.* On the flip chart, scribe *'The sun is like a ...'* and draw some of the toys which the children have suggested.

Move on to other images. Show the orange. How could it be said to look like the sun? (Colour, shape and so on.) Some young children might say that *'The sun is like an orange squirting out juice'* and go on to explain that sunlight is like *'the juice of an orange!'*

Look for other foods that look like the sun: *lemon, melon, grapefruit, pizza, birthday cake, an egg...* and so on. On the flip chart, scribe *'The sun is like ...'* and again draw in the various foods suggested.

Another rich seam for this kind of image work is to ask which flowers are like the sun. They must, of course be round and usually yellow or orange: *marigold, sunflower, buttercup, a yellow rose, daffodil, primrose.* Again use the flip chart.

With the children, read back the list poem which they have created. *'The sun is like a yellow frisbee, an orange balloon. The sun is like a crispy pizza, a juicy orange. The sun is like a golden buttercup, a sunflower climbing up the fence.'*

Finish the session by giving out the copies of photocopiable sheet 129. Ask the children to draw and colour their imaginative images of the sun in the spaces. Scribe, or ask them to copy, *The sun is like a lemon lollipop* or whatever, filling in the space with their own words to match the pictures they have drawn. Copying the ideas into lines gives a ready-made poem.

Suggestion(s) for extension
Suggest that children work in a similar pattern to make an image poem, either orally or by copying and drawing: *'The moon is like ...' 'A rainbow is like ...' 'A cloud is like ...'*

Suggestion(s) for support

Children can be encouraged to work on a single idea at a time. In relation to the sun, they should be encouraged to create images of either toys or food. Take simple one-idea images, for example: *The sun is like a biscuit. The sun is like a yellow Smartie.* Do not ask for a range of suggestions.

Assessment opportunities

This activity gives an opportunity to listen for creative language and imaginative ideas – ideas which nobody else has thought of. It can give surprising results, and often children with relatively poor language skills can think of some very original images.

Display ideas

Go for gold in this display! Encourage the use of all the vibrant colours; yellow and orange, red and gold. Cut out a round 'sun' with all the various images cut out and pasted around the edges. Scribe the poem(s) to go alongside the frieze.

Other aspects of the English PoS covered

Reading – 1d.
Writing – 1c; 2b.

Reference to photocopiable sheet

Photocopiable sheet 129 encourages the children to develop poetic ability by drawing and writing (or copying) related images into successive spaces, thus assembling a composite poem.

Performance ideas

Make orange and yellow crêpe 'sunshine' hats and have a group of children say the words of their sun poems to music (bells, chime bars and xylophone).

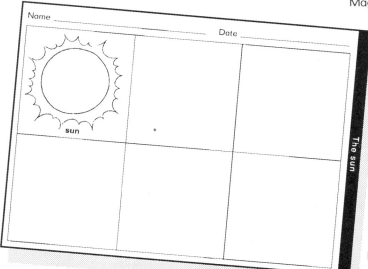

WEATHER WATCH

To enable children to explore and develop ideas connected with weather activities, with particular emphasis on using the language of the senses.

†† *Whole class or groups of any suitable size.*

⏱ *Variable, from 15–30 minutes.*

⚠ *Be aware of safety issues related to exposure to rain (cold, pollution) and sun (burning). Children must be warned not to look directly at the sun.*

Previous skills/knowledge needed

The children should be accustomed to observing and keeping a class record of the day-to-day weather.

Key background information

This activity is based on observing and talking about changes in the weather. Weather is, of course, a free but very rich resource available at any season of the year, so exploit it! Try to encourage children to think and talk 'through the senses' as this deepens and extends their descriptive language skills. This activity can be undertaken on a number of different occasions for different kinds of weather.

Preparation

Preparation depends entirely on the kind of weather. If you intend to go outside to observe, touch or even taste the weather, boots and woollen hats will be needed for snowy days, anoraks with hoods for rain. On some occasions, simply gathering round the window and looking out may provide adequate language possibilities.

Resources needed

Flip chart, pictures of different weather, weather chart or calendar, a collection of poems about different kinds of weather, for example: 'A Week of Winter Weather' by Wes Magee, from *The Witch's Brew and Other Poems* (CUP, 1989); 'Shower' by Moira Andrew, from *Madtail, Miniwhale* (Penguin, 1989); 'I am the rain' by Grace Nichols, from *Another First Poetry Book* (OUP, 1987). One copy per child of the photocopiable summative assessment sheet on page 130 (if required).

What to do

This will depend on the weather! On a sunny day, take the children out to sit in the shade of a tree. Look at and talk about the patterns made by shadows. Ask the children to make shadows with their hands and fingers. *What do they look like? Can you make a wolf, a hen, a cat?* and so on. Feel the difference between the hot sun and sitting in the shade. (Warn the children not to stay long in bright sunlight and **never** to look directly at the sun.) Feel the warmth of the outside of the school building. Talk about this and encourage the children to explore the

SPEAKING AND LISTENING

language of touch: *hot as an oven, warm as the sand in summer, cold as a fridge.*

Look at the colours of flowers and trees. Encourage the children to explore colour words: *yellow like the sun, green as the waves, bright as fireworks* and so on. Look at and discuss the kinds of clothes people wear in the sun. Use the flip chart to collect the children's sunshine language.

When it is possible and they are suitably dressed, take the children out in the rain for a few minutes. Ask them to listen to the sound it makes on the tops of litter bins, on the roof of a shed, on the grass, dropping from the trees. Does it always sound the same? Encourage them to listen to the rhythms of the rain. Make up nonsense words to go with the rain sounds: *drippety drop, drippety drop; mizzle, drizzle, plop! mizzle, drizzle, plop!* (Later, the children could play some of these rhythms on percussion instruments.)

Ask the children to feel the rain on their hands (not their faces). *It feels like: a shower with your clothes on/like you're in a waterfall/like you are in the middle of a fountain.* When you come back into the cloakroom, smell the wet coats and talk about other times when you can smell the rain, for example, after a long dry spell. Discuss what the rain is like in big cities – why is it better to avoid the rain there? (Because of pollution caused by traffic.)

Collect rain words from the children and scribe them on the flip chart: *wet, shower, pouring, splashing, pelting,* etc.

The wind makes for a lively language lesson. Let the children run into the wind and feel its strength – *like a giant pushing you.* Look at what it does to the branches of trees, to leaves in autumn, to coats and scarves and hair. Back in the classroom, talk about the fact that we can't see the wind, but we can feel and hear it and see what it does to things. *Is it like a ghost? An invisible man?* With the children's help, scribe a set of wind words and ideas on the flip chart.

Falling snow probably makes the most impact on the children. They can feel how cold it is, how it melts, how soft it is. (Warn them not to eat snow, even when it is falling.) Watch snow falling. What does it look like? *Like white butterflies/like tissue paper/like feathers?* Gather the children's snow words on the flip chart and get them to read the words back.

Finish off each session by reading weather poems to the children. Let them listen for words which they might have used or for words and phrases that are new to them. Look at and discuss the weather pictures, emphasising colour (or lack of it in a rainy day/cloudy/foggy picture). Look at the movement caused by wind and storms. Ask the children to suggest the sounds they might hear if they were in the rain/wind/storm scene.

Suggestion(s) for extension

The children can make up list poems orally, using words and ideas from the flip chart. Ask an adult to write out the poems and let the children make them into zigzag books of weather poems.

Suggestion(s) for support

When you are exploring weather language outside, try to keep the less able children near you. Draw their attention to the details and help them to experience the feel of wind, sound of rain, the look of snowflakes falling and so on. Back in the classroom, review their language ideas and any new vocabulary skills.

Assessment opportunities

This activity can be used for summative assessment, and photocopiable sheet 130 is provided for this purpose. Note the children's abilities in understanding and contributing to

Figure 6

SPEAKING AND LISTENING

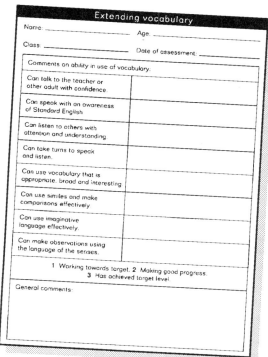

Name: _____ Age: _____

Class: _____ Date of assessment: _____

Comments on ability in use of vocabulary:	
Can talk to the teacher or other adult with confidence.	
Can speak with an awareness of Standard English	
Can listen to others with attention and understanding	
Can take turns to speak and listen.	
Can use vocabulary that is appropriate, broad and interesting	
Can use similes and make comparisons effectively	
Can use imaginative language effectively.	
Can make observations using the language of the senses.	

1 Working towards target. 2 Making good progress.
3 Has achieved target level.

General comments:

---

the work on weather images. Can they contribute an original suggestion for different weathers? (For example: *Rain is like a waterfall. Frost is when cobwebs look like lace.*) Listen for evidence (in the relevance and appropriateness of their responses) that they have listened carefully.

Display ideas
Make a large 'Weather Watch' floor book. Suggest that the children copy some of the weather poems which you have read. Ask individuals to contribute paintings of rainy/snowy/sunny days. Outline these pictures in black felt-tipped pen and glue them into the weather book, facing the appropriate poems.

Make a weather frieze. Use kites and flying leaves to decorate the wind picture; children with bright umbrellas and big boots for the rain section, plus a jagged strip of tinfoil for lightning; flowers or seaside pictures for sunshine; trees and fences silhouetted in black with lots of white paint and a red winter sun for the snow scene; grey and black shapes covered with netting for mist and fog. (See Figure 6.) Add new images to the frieze as the weather changes.

Other aspects of the English PoS covered
Reading – 1b, c; 2b.

Performance ideas
Suggest that the children make up rhythmic percussion music to go with the rain/storm/wind/snow words. These can be made into songs to go with the music, then performed to other classes in the school. The children who are performing can wear paper hats of different colours: white crêpe for snow, yellow and orange for sunshine; silver foil for rain;

blue and purple for wind; grey for thunder; gold for lightning and so on.

Reference to photocopiable sheet
Photocopiable sheet 130 can be used for summative assessment of the children's success in extending their vocabulary, based on this activity.

YESTERDAY

To give children practice in using the past tense and the language of narrative.

†† *Whole class, then several equal-sized groups.*

🕐 *20 minutes.*

Previous skills/knowledge needed
Children should be confident about talking and holding discussions in the class/group situation. They should be familiar with a range of nursery rhymes and traditional stories.

Key background information
This activity is based on made-up telephone conversations, which are in turn based on nursery rhyme situations and what some of the characters do and say in traditional tales.

Preparation
For each group, make up a 'telephone' using yoghurt pots and string or collect a number of toy telephones. Have illustrated nursery rhyme and traditional story books available.

Resources needed
Nursery rhyme books, books of traditional stories, pictures and posters of nursery rhyme characters, toy and pretend telephones, a flip chart.

What to do
Gather the children in the story corner. Make sure that they can all see you and hold up a nursery rhyme picture. Discuss who the characters are and what they are doing. For example, if you have chosen *Humpty Dumpty*, ask the children to describe him. *What is he made of? What shape is he? What is he wearing?* The children may reply: *He's an egg dressed up in clothes. He's a kind of rounded shape with little thin legs. He's got a black bow tie and a red jacket.* Encourage vivid description.

Ask two of the more articulate children to use the telephone. Suggest one reports that yesterday she saw Humpty Dumpty tumbling off the wall. She should tell what happened to her friend on the other end of the line. Explain that they should begin their conversation politely, saying who is speaking and who they want to talk to. The conversation might go along these lines: *'Hello. This is Julie. May I speak to Max, please?' 'It's Max here. Any news?'*

SPEAKING AND LISTENING

Now encourage the first child to bring the conversation round to 'what happened yesterday'. She might say something like, *'Guess what – I saw Humpty Dumpty yesterday.'* The second child should respond with *'Humpty Dumpty! What does he look like?'* or *'Where did you see him?'* or *'What was he doing?'*

Work through the conversation, encouraging the first child to describe what she imagined she saw and heard, with the second child responding. The children who are listening can make suggestions if the first two get stuck for words. They should refer to the picture for more details, if necessary.

Give several pairs the chance to practise their telephone reporting skills, using a different picture each time. It is important that you emphasise that the imaginary meeting took place *yesterday* (or last week or last month), so that the children are forced into using the past tense.

Put the children into several equal-sized groups, giving each group a 'telephone' to work with. The groups should each choose a story or a nursery rhyme picture on which to base their conversation.

After five minutes or so, bring the groups back together and have them act out their telephone conversations. They should take the parts of those making the calls, for example: a newspaper reporter phoning in his 'copy', a nosy neighbour, Humpty Dumpty's old granny, a horrified teacher telling another member of staff about Mary bringing a lamb to school.

If you think the narrative description could be made more graphic, be ready to ask questions to make the children think: *'What was the wolf wearing?'* *'What did Little Red Riding Hood have in her basket?'* *'What happened to Grandma?'* and so on.

Suggestion(s) for extension

Give the children the opportunity to work out a different scenario, realistic or fantastic, for their telephone conversations. *'Guess what! I met a Martian yesterday!'* *'I spoke to the Man in the Moon!'* *'I met the singer from Blur yesterday!'*

Suggestion(s) for support

Have a more articulate child working with one who needs support. The less able child should describe what happened, what he saw, etc. The other can ask helpful questions to move the conversation along.

Assessment opportunities

Note the children who are able/unable to use the past tense correctly.

Display ideas

On a backing frieze, create a town scene with a number of human figures painted and cut out. These figures should each be using a telephone box or a mobile phone. At the other end of the frieze, create a second scene in the countryside where an equal number of figures are using phones. String the phones to a telegraph pole in the middle of the frieze, so that there is a web of string going from one set of characters to the other. (See illustration below.)

Make a wall-sized 'newspaper' with reports and 'photographs' (black and white paintings or pen drawings) in columns of the various story-book scenarios which have been acted out as telephone conversations.

Other aspects of the English PoS covered

Reading – 1b, d.
Writing – 1b; 2b.

Performance ideas

Ask the children to act out their telephone conversations between nursery rhyme or story-book characters for other children in the school. These can be improvised as dramas.

Information handling

We live in a world where vast amounts of information are created, disseminated, analysed and stored. Our children, therefore, must be given the skills with which to handle and pass on information in an informed and ordered way.

This section aims to help children use forms of directed language which will enable their listeners to follow instructions and carry out a number of simple tasks. The speakers should be able to explain and inform, and the listeners to respond, using the skills of 'reactive listening'. Some of the activities suggested will enable children to describe a process using the language of sequencing; others are designed to encourage children to speak with confidence in front of a group or to converse in a self-reliant way with an adult.

Too often, we hear adults who are unable or unwilling to offer a simple explanation of something, or who find it difficult to express their opinions in public. The *Information handling* activities are designed to give children practice in these language skills, so that they can develop confidence in speaking aloud and in using directed language in the non-threatening environment of the classroom.

FRAMED!

To help children gain confidence in speaking in front of a group audience. To enable them to respond to factual questions.

†† *Whole class or group.*

🕐 *20 minutes.*

Previous skills/knowledge needed

It is helpful if the children already know their own age and address.

Key background information

'Framed!' is intended as a very early activity, probably taking place during the first week at school. It can be looked on as a 'Getting to know you' game.

Preparation

Make badges printed with the children's first names (sticky-backed labels are ideal), and a card 'picture frame' big enough to go round a child's face.

Resources needed

Keep the class register handy so that you can help the children who have forgotten or do not know their address. You can also check on the children's birth dates. Make one copy per child of photocopiable sheet 131.

What to do

Sit the children comfortably in the reading/listening corner and tell them that they are going to play a 'Getting to know you' game.

Frame your own face to show the children how they will look 'framed'. Only the person framed answers questions. Choose a fairly confident child to go first. Ask, 'Are you a boy or a girl?' Encourage a one-sentence formula answer: not just 'Girl', but 'I am a girl.'

After asking a few questions of your own to set the scene, get other children to join in. Encourage factual questions of the 'What is your name?' 'What age are you?' and 'Where do you live?' variety, checking that everyone knows their own address. The formula approach, 'My name is...' 'I live at...' makes it easier for those children who lack confidence. Give the children a name badge or sticker to wear after answering questions. Give out copies of photocopiable sheet 131, and ask the children to write in appropriate facts about themselves and their family members. Assist with writing if necessary.

Suggestion(s) for extension

When children have shown that they are capable of answering the simple formula questions suggested above, move on to asking them questions about brothers and sisters: their names and ages, their place in the family (oldest, youngest and so on).

Get those children to go on to describe the house they live in: the house number, colour of the front door, what they can see from their bedroom window and so on.

Suggestion(s) for support

Invite another adult (nursery helper, parent, ancillary) to work with the less confident children on a one-to-one basis, helping them to learn their correct address.

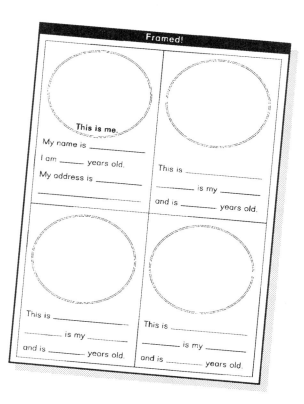

Assessment opportunities

Use the children's work on photocopiable sheet 131 to note which children can and cannot answer the name, age and address questions accurately.

Listen for those who speak in a confident manner and note those who will need extra help to speak out with confidence.

Display ideas

Give the children A4 size art/sugar paper and ask them to paint their own portrait so that their face fills the paper. When the paintings are dry, they can be cut out and pasted collage-style, with speech balloons bearing each child's name. Put a frame around the whole frieze and entitle it *Framed!* or *Here we are in school!*

Other aspects of the English PoS covered

Reading – 1b; 2b, e.
Writing – 1b.

Reference to photocopiable sheet

Photocopiable sheet 131 is an assessment sheet which requires the children to present basic information about themselves and their relations in a formal style.

I SPY

To give children practice in auditory discrimination.
†† *Whole class.*
🕐 *Five minutes or so, which can be fitted into odd moments of the daily routine.*

Previous skills/knowledge needed

The children should have had some experience in 'key phonic' (that is, listening for and recognition of the first sound of a word).

Key background information

Because the children have to listen attentively to be able to identify separate sounds, this activity can be used to reinforce early listening skills. It can also be used to reinforce the courtesy expected of them in taking turns to speak.

Preparation

Make alphabet cards with a single letter on each.

Resources needed

A selection of illustrated alphabet books.

What to do

Choose one child to start the game off. Holding up the correct alphabet card, he or she should say: *I spy with my little eye something beginning with* [for example] *b*.

The other children put their hands up and take turns to guess what the object is: *Is it a bin? Is it the blackboard? Is it a book?* and so on, until the object is guessed.

Then the game is handed on, the successful guesser taking a different alphabet card and setting the next *I spy* question.

Look at the 'b' page pictures in the alphabet books with the children. Ask them to find more words beginning with 'b'. Reinforce their phonic listening skills by using the appropriate pages in the alphabet books, again using the *I spy* formula.

This activity can be played time and again, in odd moments before home-time or while waiting to go to assembly.

Suggestion(s) for extension

When the children become more experienced in playing the *I spy* game, let them choose an unseen object, in the hall or in the school grounds, for example. Make sure that they choose something that most of the others will know about although they can not see it from where they are: *gate, tree, climbing frame,* for example.

I spy is an ideal game to play on the coach or train going to and from an outside visit. In this context, the children may increase the complexity of the game by referring to objects which the vehicle has just passed and which are no longer visible.

Suggestion(s) for support

Children who find this activity difficult can be helped by an adult working with them in a small group. The adult should work first from the alphabet books before moving on to looking for objects. She could also take the activity at a much slower pace, stressing the need for listening to the key sound and reducing the competitive element in the game.

SPEAKING AND
LISTENING

left without disturbance until the seeds begin to grow. It should be easily accessible to the monitoring group.

Resources needed

Empty eggshells (without their 'lids') – one per group, a packet of mustard and cress seeds, Blu-Tack, felt-tipped pens, cotton wool or potting compost, an old spoon, a jug, one copy per child of photocopiable sheet 132.

What to do

Take the group to the newspaper-covered table. Assemble the eggshells, a jug of water, cotton wool and seeds. Let them carefully use felt-tipped pens to draw a funny face on the shell. Get them to suggest a different name for each one: *Harry Egg, Henrietta Egg, Eddie Egg* and so on.

Put some moist cotton wool or potting compost in each eggshell. Stand the shells upright, fixing them in position with a blob of Blu-Tack. Plant quite a few mustard and cress seeds in each one. Keep the cotton wool or compost moist, but do not over-water, until the egg's 'hair' begins to grow.

When the eggs have a good crop of hair, let the children talk through the process, first in their own group. When they are happy that they can explain to others, let them show off their finished product, then describe the ingredients. Encourage them to tell what steps they took, in what order, to make their egg's hair grow. Get the listeners to ask questions: *What happened next? How long did the hair take to grow?* so that they are actively taking part in the speaking/ listening process.

Give out the copies of photocopiable sheet 132. The children can use this to illustrate and label the steps in the process of growing the 'hair' on the egg. (See 'Reference to photocopiable sheet' below for details.) The completed sheet can be used as the basis of a sequencing zigzag book.

Assessment opportunities

This activity readily indicates children whose phonic listening is well-developed and those who need more practice. After spending a few minutes on 'I spy' as a class activity, it may be a good idea to divide the children into ability groups, so that those who are less confident have more time to think about words beginning with a particular sound and are not drowned out by others who are more capable.

Display ideas

Ask the children to do some felt-tipped pen drawings of the letters of the alphabet. Then they can cut out some magazine pictures relevant to each letter and assemble these, collage-fashion, alongside their drawings to make alphabet books.

Another way of displaying 'I spy with my little eye' is to make large cut-out letters, covering each with the appropriate drawings and pictures, as shown in the illustration.

Other aspects of the English PoS covered

Reading – 1c; 2b.

Writing – 2d.

Suggestion(s) for extension

Try other simple experiments of this kind, letting each group in turn take part. They could try growing runner beans, grass hair on a potato head, or growing mustard and cress in other containers (orange or grapefruit skins, for example).

Get the children to talk through the process, beginning with the ingredients required. As they are talking, scribe the ingredients and then the process onto a flip chart or whiteboard. Read it back to them, asking them to listen with their eyes closed. If they think you have made a mistake or put things out of order, get them to raise their hands so that you can change it.

▣◆ HARRY EGG'S HAIR

To encourage children to describe a process accurately to others.

†† *Groups of six to eight children.*

◔ *The experiment will take a week to ten days, the ensuing language work about 30 minutes.*

Previous skills/knowledge needed

Children should be aware that water, light and air help seeds to grow into plants.

Key background information

This activity needs to be well-organised and the children motivated to sustain their interest over a period of time.

Preparation

Cover a table with newspaper before beginning this activity. Make sure that there is an area where the eggshells can be

Suggestion(s) for support

Put those children who have difficulty in remembering a complete process in one working group and get them to perform and talk about just the part they themselves took. If the group members then speak in order, the whole process can be successfully relayed to the others.

SPEAKING AND LISTENING

Assessment opportunities

Observe the children's awareness of sequencing, noting those who can follow the process through from start to finish and those who can remember only one or two parts in isolation.

Opportunities for IT

Older and more able children could use a word processor to write the instructions for growing the egg's hair. They should originate their work on the screen and then check it through with another child or adult to make sure they have the instructions in the right order. If they have pieces of text out of order, they should be shown how to mark and move the line rather than delete it and type it out again.

An alternative activity for older children could be for the teacher to create a word-processed file giving the instructions in the wrong order. The children could then be asked to sort them out by marking and moving the lines, using either a 'cut and paste' (where the text is deleted and then copied back in) or a 'drag and drop' (where the marked line is dragged to the new position using the mouse).

Younger children who are not yet writing independently could use a concept keyboard linked to the word processor. A prepared overlay could have the different parts of the activity in the wrong order. By pressing appropriate points on the overlay, the sections can be displayed on the screen in the correct order, and the final version printed out.

Display ideas

Make a wall chart recipe, zigzag-style, for growing Harry Egg's hair. If the children can copy or are at the stage of independent writing, they can write it out themselves. Otherwise, scribe it on their behalf. The children should illustrate each part of the process.

Other aspects of the English PoS covered
Reading – 1c; 2c.
Writing – 1a, c; 2b.

Reference to photocopiable sheet

Use photocopiable sheet 132 to make individual zigzag books, one illustration on each page in sequence. In box 1 of the sheet, the children can draw the relevant ingredients (seeds, cotton wool and so on). In box 2, they can give the

egg a face. In box 3, they can show new seedlings and a jug of water. In box 4, they can show the egg with lots of green hair.

Performance ideas

When the growing experiments are finished, encourage the children to explain the process to an audience, perhaps at assembly in the school hall.

LIKES AND DISLIKES

To encourage children to go beyond one-word answers to questions.
†† *Whole class or group.*
🕐 *10–15 minutes.*

Previous skills/knowledge needed

The children should know the names of each of their five senses.

Key background information

This activity requires no particular resources and no specific preparation.

What to do

Ask the children to think about two things they like and two things they do not like. Suggest first that they concentrate on things to eat. Children like talking about food, and they tend to find it an easy starting point for putting forward a personal opinion. Most children have strong likes and dislikes connected with food and it is an area of common experience. They may say, 'I like sausages, but I don't like cabbage.'

SPEAKING AND
LISTENING

Ask, for example, 'Why do you like sausages?' Encourage the children to think about, for example, taste and smell when giving their answers. Suggest that the next child poses the question 'Why don't you like cabbage?', always encouraging full questions and full answers.

Explore the way children feel about food through their senses – for example, the crunchy feel of biting into an apple, the sound of sausages popping in the pan, the smell of newly-baked cakes, the look of shiny cherries, the tangy taste of a ripe tangerine. This language work builds on the children's personal experience and helps them to extend their answers in an interesting and creative way.

Suggestion(s) for extension

Suggest that the children move on to expressing opinions about other things they do or do not like, for example, why they like (or do not like) wearing school clothes, television programmes they like or do not like – and why.

Make up a short list poem with the children, scribing their ideas about liking and disliking foods based on their exploration of the senses. Use the flip chart or whiteboard. The poem might run along these lines:

> I like the taste of sausages.
> I like to hear them sizzle in the pan.
> I like the smell of sausages.
> I like to watch them popping
> in the pan.
>
> I don't like the taste of cabbage.
> I don't like eating green things.
> I don't like the smell of cabbage.
> I don't like the feel of it in my mouth.
> Cabbage feels like seaweed.

Scribe the finished poem onto a wall chart, so that the children can 'read' it back aloud the next day. This encourages recognition of the written phrases 'I like' and 'I don't like'.

Suggestion(s) for support

Put the children into two groups, I like and I don't like. Those in the first group should tell the others about one thing they really like; those in the second group should tell the others about one thing they do not like. This way, every child has a starting point, for example, 'I like cheeseburgers.' 'I don't like sprouts.' This 'starter' helps those who are finding it difficult to express their opinion orally. Once they are happy with the simple phrase, it can be extended by asking the question 'Why?'

Assessment opportunities

Listen for children whose language is limited and who find it difficult to go beyond the simple opening phrase. Compare

their language with those who can express an opinion and give reasons.

Opportunities for IT

The children could use an art package to draw something that they like or dislike. The resulting picture could be used as a part of the class display.

Figure 1

Display ideas

Ask the children to paint one thing they enjoy eating and one that they do not like. When the pictures are dry, cut out and mount them collage-style in two different 'shop fronts', barrows or baskets. Call one *'We like'* and the other *'We don't like'*. Ask for 'enjoyment' words, for example, *scrumptious, delicious, tasty* and 'don't like' words, *disgusting, yukky, horrid* and so on. Print word cards to place around the two displays (see Figure 1).

Make simple-fold books of four pages using one sheet of A4 (see Figure 2). Have the children copy the phrase *'I like'* with one word and a picture beneath it. Title the book *My I Like Book*.

Figure 2

Other aspects of the English PoS covered
Reading – 1c.
Writing – 1b, c; 2b.

Performance ideas

The children can recite the list poem in two groups, the *We like* group and the *We don't like* group (or the *Yum* group and the *Yuk* group), each child stepping forward to say a single line. Let the children hold up the real food or a painted

cut-out of it. Make up a chorus for the like/don't like word sets so that the whole group joins in at the end of each three lines, for example:

Food wonderful food,
scrumptious, delicious, tasty food,
things we love to eat!

Food revolting food,
horrid, yukky, disgusting food,
things we hate to eat!

DIFFERENT HATS

To provide children with an opportunity to speak in front of a group.

†† *A group of six to eight children. When they are ready, the children will present their ideas to the whole class.*

🕐 *30 minutes.*

Key background information

This activity needs careful management. It may be the first time that the children have been asked to explore other people's lives and characters in an imaginative way. An 'inside knowledge' of the stories and television programmes currently enthralling the children will help you to suggest characters for those who need help in making a choice.

Preparation

To get this activity off to a good start, select the first group from children who have a lot to say for themselves.

Resources needed

One copy per child of photocopiable sheet 133. A collection of hats: a traffic warden's cap, a nurse's cap, a bowler, a fancy wedding hat, a school uniform cap or hat, a flat cap, a motorcycle helmet. The hats should be as diverse as possible.

What to do

Suggest that each child in the group chooses a hat to make them into a 'different person' – give them a new identity. The children should choose new names to go with the hats. They can even take on magical or fantastic identities!

Take time to work with the group who are presenting the oral work first. By asking questions and making suggestions, help them to think of names and situations for their new characters, building on current story and television favourites.

Wearing their hats – and their new identities! – the group should stand in front of the other children (whose turn will come later). They should talk as though the hats had made them into different people. Encourage them to use different voices as well.

They should tell three things about themselves, for example:

'I am a giant. My name is Boris. I ride across the mountains on an elephant's back.'

Once each child has finished speaking, the listeners should be allowed to ask one question each and the child should answer in her or his new persona. For example, they may wish to know if the elephant is a giant too.

▲ 'What size is your elephant, Boris?'
▲ 'My elephant is as big as the school hall.'
▲ 'What colour is your elephant, Boris?'
▲ 'My elephant wears a patchwork coat like Elmer.'
▲ 'What does he like to eat?'
▲ 'My elephant likes to eat cheese on toast.' and so on.

Try to get the listeners to listen carefully to the questions that have gone before, so that there is a different question each time.

Use photocopiable sheet 133 to discuss with the children who might wear each kind of hat shown in the pictures. Discuss the functions these hats have (safety, recognition, hygiene and so on). Suggest that they use the empty space to draw a hat for someone doing a special job (for example, a spaceman's helmet) and explain why this hat is necessary for the job.

Suggestion(s) for extension

This work can be extended across several days. Make the hats available in the home base, and suggest that the children talk to one another informally, each in her or his new identity. This will encourage inventive play.

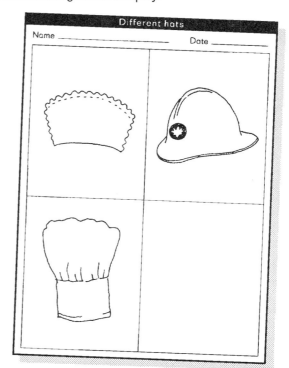

SPEAKING AND LISTENING

Suggestion(s) for support

Pair a confident child with one who is less so. Let each choose a hat, spending five minutes listening and talking to one another in character.

Assessment opportunities

During the question time, listen to the kinds of questions asked and answers given. Are they imaginative? Do they fit the character? Do they move the conversation or story on?

Display ideas

Ask each child to make a picture of a hat, collage-style, using materials (scraps of velvet, silk, lace and feathers) or a variety of different papers. All the hats should be more or less life-size. Make a hat shop window frieze and display each hat on a stand. (See illustration below.)

Other aspects of the English PoS covered

Reading – 1b, c.

Reference to photocopiable sheet

Photocopiable sheet 133 shows three hats which are associated with particular jobs. These pictures are used as a resource for discussion. In the fourth (empty) space the child can draw another type of hat, leading to further explanation.

Performance ideas

Wearing the hats and in character, the children should tell those in another class all about themselves, their names, where they live, what they like to eat, what pets they have and so on. This will extend the imaginative activity and stretch their storytelling abilities.

SECRET PLACES

To enable children to use descriptive language with accuracy and attention to detail.

†† *Small groups of four or five.*

🕐 *30 minutes.*

⚠ *Outdoor work should be supervised by an adult.*

Previous skills/knowledge needed

The children should be familiar with using a tape recorder.

Key background information

The ability to use detailed descriptive language is an important skill which needs to be consciously developed.

Preparation

Put a cassette in the cassette player and set it so that the children need only press the button marked 'record' to begin their task.

Resources needed

Cassette player (with microphone), cassette. One copy per child of the photocopiable summative assessment sheet on page 134 (if required).

What to do

Explain to one group that they should go out into the school grounds (accompanied by a classroom assistant or parent helper) and find a 'secret' place. Once they have collectively decided on the place, they should look around it as if they had not been there before. Ask them what is special about the place, what colours they see, what they can hear and so on.

When they have decided who should say what, they should switch on the cassette player (in recording mode) and describe what they can see and hear – *without giving away the actual location*. (They may need to keep back key bits of information.)

If they decide that their secret place is the school garden, they may say:

▲ 'We can't see the front door from here, but we can see the corner of Mrs Webb's classroom.'
▲ 'We can hear the nursery children playing on their slide.'
▲ 'We can hear some birds tweeting.'
▲ 'We can see grass and we can see the fence.'
▲ 'There are lots of blue flowers.'
▲ 'Where are we?'

Back in the classroom, the group should replay their recording. The other children should try to guess where the secret place is from the clues given. Do not let the children shout out their guesses: they must put up their hands when they think they know. Ask those in the 'secret place' group to choose who answers, letting each child have one turn only.

SPEAKING AND LISTENING

Discuss the descriptions of the secret place with the whole class. What do they think was the best clue? Is there any other place in the school grounds where you can see the fence and grass at the same time? What else might they have said they could hear from there? How accurate do the others think the clues were?

Choose a second group to go off and find a secret place. They should go through the same procedure, look around, listen and then put their clues on tape.

Suggestion(s) for extension
Let another group choose something familiar from the classroom: a pencil sharpener, the register, a calculator. They must not give away the name of the object, but describe it accurately on tape so that the others can guess what it is.

Develop this activity into creating an imaginary secret place. The children can work in pairs, one child describing his secret place, the other drawing what she thinks it looks like. This extension stretches the children's descriptive language skills.

Those children who are writing independently may like to write stories set in their secret place. A large zigzag format, lavishly illustrated, is ideal for this activity.

Suggestion(s) for support
Let a child who has difficulty in articulating her or his description work with one other child. They should stand back to back, each describing one thing that they can see. They should change places and say if what the other child said was correct. Then they can choose one other thing, stopping each time to check the accuracy of the description. When they have thought of and checked three things, they should record them on a cassette before getting another pair to guess where they were standing.

Information handling

Name _____ Age _____

Class: _____ Date of assessment: _____

Comments on ability in handling information.

Can work effectively with other children.	
Can talk to the teacher or other adult with confidence.	
Can speak with an awareness of Standard English.	
Can take turns to speak and listen.	
Can present simple factual information in an organised way.	
Can listen to and interpret spoken information.	
Can offer relevant descriptions based on observation.	

1 Working towards target. 2 Making good progress.
3 Has achieved target level.

General comments:

Assessment opportunities
This activity can be used for summative asessment, and photocopiable sheet 134 is provided for this purpose. Note the children's awareness of their surroundings and their ability to use appropriate words to describe their location. Listen for evidence (in the relevance and appropriateness of their responses) that they have listened carefully.

Opportunities for IT
The children's use of a cassette player to record their own descriptions involves them in controlling an everyday device, and should be seen as a part of their IT experience. Encourage them to rewind the tape to listen to their work, possibly editing and re-recording it. They may need to be shown how to use the fast forward and rewind buttons and the counter, so that they can return to parts of the tape quickly. Make sure they can use the pause button; and, if they are using a remote microphone, that they can use the microphone button to stop and start their recording.

Display ideas
Get the children to draw, paint or colour and cut out their imagined secret places. Paste them on to an appropriate background: an island, a forest, outer space. Label the finished picture *Our secret places*.

Other aspects of the English PoS covered
Writing – 1a, b, c; 2a, b.

Reference to photocopiable sheet
Photocopiable sheet 134 can be used for summative assessment of the children's information handling skills, based on this activity.

SURPRISE, SURPRISE!

To encourage children to use accurate and vivid description based on the sense of touch.

†† *Whole class.*

🕐 *20 minutes.*

Previous skills/knowledge needed

It is useful, but not strictly necessary, that the children should have some experience with the language of imagery.

Key background knowledge

Help the children towards accurate and vivid description by your questions. This activity is a way in to working on descriptive written language, so it is useful to keep this spin-off in mind.

Preparation

Gather the objects in a deep box or bag. Wrap one of them in a silk scarf before getting the children together.

Resources needed

A variety of unusual objects, (a button hook, a fan, a precious stone, a paperweight) previously unseen by the children, a deep box or bag, a silk (or silk-like) scarf.

What to do

Gather the children around you and tell them that you have some surprises in the bottom of the box/bag. Suggest that it is to be a kind of guessing game. Make it all very mysterious. Slowly, with the air of a magician, take the wrapped-up object out of the box/bag. Ask if anyone would like to hold it. Let a child handle the object, still wrapped.

Make the point that she should not say what she thinks the object is, but ask her to say something about how it feels. Give the child a moment or so to answer, then pass the object on.

Ask the children open questions as the object is passed from hand to hand. For example, if the first object is a paperweight, ask:

▲ What shape do you think it is?

▲ How heavy do you think it is?

▲ What do you think it is made of?

Encourage the children to expand their answers, not saying simply *'round'*, but *'round on the top'*, *'round like a ball on the top'*, *'flat with a place to put your thumb underneath'*. And *'heavy as a cricket ball'*, *'heavy as a stone'*. Then they can do some guesswork: *'made of something shiny like a door knob on a church door'*, *'made of a slippery stone'* and so on – all without sight of the object itself.

Once the object has been unwrapped, there may be colours and patterns to talk about and all kinds of suggestions about what it might be used for. Work in the same way with several other hidden objects.

As a follow-on to the purely oral work, scribe some of the children's descriptive suggestions in list form on a flip chart or whiteboard.

The list could begin to take the shape of a poem. For example, the description of the paperweight might look like this:

Surprise, surprise!
Round and shiny as a door knob,
heavy as a stone on the shore,
shining like ice in the sun,
the surprise has purple flowers
trapped inside like butterflies.
What is it?

Let the children copy the poem inside an opening riddle book (see Figure 3). They can print the answer under the flap.

Suggestion(s) for extension

Place an unwrapped object in the box/bag and let the children close their eyes and 'dig for treasure' at the bottom of the

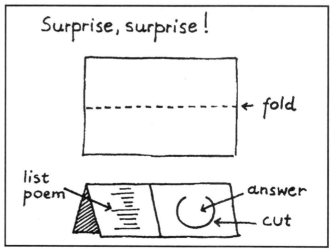

Figure 3

SPEAKING AND LISTENING

box/bag. Encourage them to talk about the feel of the object they find hidden there. From their description, the other children have to guess what the object might be.

Suggest that each child brings in a surprise object from home. This should be wrapped up and presented to the other children as part of the 'Surprise, surprise!' game. Show that you treat these 'treasures' with great respect and that you expect all the children to take care with them.

Suggestion(s) for support
Give the children who find 'touch words' difficult a set of ordinary things to feel, asking them to make sets of rough/smooth/furry/shiny objects. Working in a similar way, move on to give them practice in classifying objects by shape until they have built up a range of descriptive touch words.

Assessment opportunities
Listen to the children's descriptive language. Note those who have difficulty with touch, colour or shape words, and offer support as suggested above.

Display ideas
After the children have explored the set of objects with their hands, eyes and in descriptive language, place the objects on a display table, using drapes of different textures, plants (some of which should have prickly leaves, some smooth), pictures, books and labels. Using scraps of velvet, sand paper, silk and wool, make a texture collage picture to go with this display. Encourage the children to talk about the

objects on display to members of other classes in the school. They should ask them to feel the texture frieze, emphasising the use of 'touch' language, perhaps using some of the new vocabulary which they have learned.

Other aspects of the English PoS covered
Reading – 1c.
Writing – 1c; 2a, b.

TEDDY BEARS' PICNIC

To enable children to include relevant detail in descriptions based on their observations.

†† *Whole class.*

⏰ *20 minutes.*

⚠ *Be aware of any food allergies or dietary restrictions; change the recipes if necessary.*

Key background information
You should be familiar with the song 'The Teddy Bears' Picnic'.

Preparation
Arrange for the children to bring their favourite soft toy or teddy bear to school. (It is a good idea to stick a name label on the back of each toy in case there is a mix-up.) Set out a picnic in the reading/listening area. If it is to be a 'real' picnic, you will need to supply biscuits, orange juice and so on.

SPEAKING AND LISTENING

Teddy bears' picnic

Chocolate muesli crunch

Makes about 30 biscuits.

Ingredients:
225g (8oz) cooking chocolate
500g (1lb 2oz) fruit and nut muesli

You will need:
paper cases, saucepan, bowl, baking tray.

This recipe needs adult supervision.

Break up the chocolate. Melt it in a bowl held over a saucepan of hot water. Remove from heat and leave to cool for a few minutes.

Stir in some muesli, until the mixture is just held together by the chocolate. Spoon the mixture into small paper cases and leave on a baking tray to cool, then refrigerate until set.

Vanilla creams

Makes about 30 sweets.

Ingredients:
1 egg white
360g (12oz) icing sugar
a few drops vanilla essence (or other flavouring)

You will need:
a board, a whisk, a bowl, a knife (not too sharp), a wooden spoon.

Whisk the egg white until frothy. Sieve the icing sugar to remove lumps. Using the wooden spoon, gradually beat about two-thirds of the icing sugar (a bit at a time) into the egg white. Add vanilla essence to taste (do not use too much, or it will taste horrible).

Spoon the mixture onto a board and knead in the rest of the icing sugar. Divide the mixture in half and shape each half into a long cylinder. Chop into roughly half a centimetre thick slices. Roll each slice into a ball. Leave to set in the refrigerator.

Resources needed

Picture story books about bears, tape of 'The Teddy Bears' Picnic' (for instance, on the cassette *20 All Time Junior Hits*, EMI), picnic basket, dolls' house teaset, one copy per child of photocopiable sheet 135, ingredients for recipes (see page 135). The BBC cassette *Teddy Tales and Rhymes* might be useful for introducing or developing the theme.

What to do

Get the children to sit round the 'picnic area' with their teddy or soft toy on their knees.

Listen to the 'Teddy Bears' Picnic' song on tape. Suggest that because the bears don't know one another, the children have to introduce them by talking about them.

Ask a confident child to begin, answering fairly simple questions:
▲ What is your bear's name?
▲ How long has he lived with you?
▲ Where does he sleep at night?

Find out if there is a story connected with the toy – if it was lost on a bus, dropped into a rock pool at the seaside, chewed by the dog.

Encourage all the children to take part. Turn the picnic into a listening lesson, with the bears learning from the children how to sit quietly while a bear story is read to them.

The children could listen to the 'Teddy Bears' Picnic' song again and then join in.

Encourage the children to talk about what kind of food makes the ideal picnic and what is unsuitable, for example, chocolate and chocolate biscuits get too messy, ice-cream

melts and so on. Make up a teddy bears' picnic menu on the flip chart or whiteboard, drawing and labelling each item.

With adult helpers, make up uncooked sweets and biscuits from the recipes on page 135.

Suggestion(s) for extension

Work with a group. Give each child a different toy hidden inside a bag: a rattle, a car, a jointed snake. Get them to look inside, then to try and describe the toy to the others (without naming it) so that they can guess what it is. If the child has a problem, help out by asking about colour, shape, who the object belongs to and so on.

Suggestion(s) for support

Put the children in pairs, each with her or his own soft toy. Get each child to tell the other child three things about her or his toy, then ask them to pass these three comments on to you or another adult. This means that a child who finds speaking aloud difficult will be talking, not for herself or himself, but for someone else; this is often an easier task.

Assessment opportunities

This activity offers an informal check on an individual child's ability to speak out with confidence. It also shows whether they are articulate and able to use descriptive language.

Display ideas

Make the classroom into a forest with tall painted trees with lots of leaves painted in a range of greens, cut out and stapled

SPEAKING AND LISTENING

on the branches, so that they hang from the walls and ceiling. Paint a checked tablecloth, cutting out and sticking pictures of food and drinks on it, collage-style. Each child should paint and cut out their own teddy or soft toy and place it on the picnic frieze.

Make a display of bears and appropriate books on the bookcases and worktops until home time. Photograph the 'picnic'.

Other aspects of the English PoS covered
Reading – 1b, d.
Writing – 1c; 2b.

Reference to photocopiable sheet
Photocopiable sheet 135 provides simple recipes for sweets and biscuits. The children can prepare these for the teacher (or another adult) to cook.

Performance ideas
Suggest that the children learn the words to 'The Teddy Bears' Picnic'. One group could sing while others mime the actions.

THE JUNK-BOX MONSTER

To enable children to describe a process, using the language of sequencing.

†† *Small groups.*

🕐 *Time needed to make the monster will vary; time involved in the speaking/listening activity 15–20 minutes.*

⚠ *Use of adhesives must be closely supervised.*

Previous skills/knowledge needed
It is useful if the children have some previous experience of building and model-making with junk materials. They need to have knowledge of what pastes/adhesives are best to use for different materials.

Key background information
This activity is an excellent way of introducing children to the skills of sequencing – not just in terms of following a process, but in terms of storytelling and book-making.

Preparation
Make sure your activity area is set up with a range of materials – boxes, different kinds of paste and adhesive and so on. Cover the working area with newspaper and ensure that the children's clothes are protected.

Resources needed
Boxes of different shapes and sizes, sticky tape, strong adhesive (for example, Copydex), paste, poster paint, a selection of junk from the junk-box.

What to do
Talk with the group about how they might go about making a monster from the materials available. Suggest that they choose the largest box for the body. Leave them with a given time to produce the completed model.

Tell them that they should try to remember what they did first: added, glued on or painted. In their group, they should talk through the making sequence, using sequential words and phrases of this kind: *'First we...' 'Then we...' 'The next thing was...' 'When we were finished ...'*

The group of makers should then explain to the others how they built their monster, consciously using the language of sequencing.

This should be regarded as a two-way activity, the listeners being able to ask questions as the process is being explained. It might go like this:
▲ 'Meet Fred, our junk-box monster.'
▲ 'What is he made of?'
▲ 'Three boxes, some string and two buttons.'
▲ 'What did you do first?'
▲ 'First we decided to get a big box for his head.'
And so on, remembering the language of sequence which the children have been practising.

Suggestion(s) for extension
The children could move from factual reporting to the realm of the imagination. Ask one group to think about a 'story' to go along with their monster – his name, where he lives, what he likes to eat and so on. Encourage the group to share ideas, listening and talking in turn. When they are satisfied

SPEAKING AND
LISTENING

with the monster's story, the group should gather together with the rest of the items and be ready to answer questions about it. Give the children five minutes to accomplish this task.

Meanwhile, the other children should be thinking about the questions they will ask: what the monster likes to eat, who his friends are and if he has any pets. The conversation might go like this:

▲ 'Where does Fred live?'
▲ 'Under the Taff bridge.'
▲ 'Who are his friends?'
▲ 'He has no friends. He is a lonely monster.'

The group of makers can now tell the monster's story in sequence.

Suggestion(s) for support
Those children who have difficulty in remembering the sequence of making might be given cards marked 1, 2, 3, 4. They can hold these cards up in order, each explaining what happened at one stage in the making of the monster.

Assessment opportunities
Listen for the children who have a command of the language of sequence. Do they use and understand 'First...' 'And then...' 'Afterwards...' 'Next...' 'When we were finished...'? Make a tick sheet headed with similar phrases.

Display ideas
Make a table display of the finished monsters, perhaps building a 'habitat' in which they live. Label the monsters by placing name tags around their necks. Make a chart for each monster to show the making sequence. (You might show the children a step-by-step recipe in pictorial form to give them the idea.)

Other aspects for the English PoS covered
Reading – 1b, d; 2c.
Writing – 1a.

WELCOME TO CLASS 2

To give children an opportunity to converse confidently with an adult.

†† *Work with whole class to establish a welcoming routine, though each welcoming 'committee' might consist of only two children.*

⏰ *The preparatory discussion may take 45 minutes, the welcome about 10 minutes.*

Previous skills/knowledge needed
The children should have some knowledge of the courtesies of getting to know someone.

Key background information
It is important to stress that, although the visitor may not be known to the children, he or she is known to the school, and that the children should not approach an unknown adult as a potential 'visitor'.

Preparation
Make a badge for each of the children. Take the children on a tour round the school to familiarise them with the staffroom, the secretary's office and so on.

Resources needed
A length of strong kitchen paper, long enough to make a welcome banner. Outline the letters WELCOME TO OUR SCHOOL. One essential resource is the class visitor! You might invite senior citizens who live nearby or adults who were pupils of the school. Invite poets, artists, dieticians, safety experts from the railway, police constables, fire fighters, the school nurse.

What to do
As soon as you know a visitor is due to come into your class, make preparations with the children to welcome her or him. Tell them who this visitor is and give an outline of the kind of thing she or he is likely to do: tell a story, read and write poems, show a special art technique, talk about how to keep healthy.

SPEAKING AND LISTENING

visitor the banner and tell her or him how it was made.

Discuss with those who will not be part of the welcoming committee some questions that they may like to ask – for example, of a visiting writer:

▲ When did you first start to write?

▲ Which book/poem did you like best when you were at school?

▲ How did you feel when you saw your first book?

▲ What is the best way to start a poem?

Choose confident children who would like to put a question to the visitor. The first questions can be those which the children have already discussed, but encourage them to ask follow-up questions if there is time and the visitor is happy to talk.

Review the visit with the children after the guest has gone, asking them to think about the most interesting things she or he said and why, and what they learned from her or him.

Suggestion(s) for extension

Get the two children who formed the 'welcoming committee' to share their experience of welcoming a visitor to school, telling the others what happened and what they learned.

Try to organise another visit of this kind, perhaps asking a grandparent who is interested in gardening, cooking or pigeon racing to talk to the children. Again, discuss with the children what questions they might ask to find out more about the visitor's hobby/interest. Ask a different pair to form the 'welcoming committee' this time. If this activity is repeated and expanded, the children will become confident in talking with adults.

Suggestion(s) for support

Pair a confident child with one who is less so and choose this couple to take on the welcoming role with a regular visitor.

Assessment opportunities

Make sure that everyone has an opportunity to act as host/hostess. Listen to the ease, or otherwise, with which they talk with the adult. Try to find out which children can make a response to the visitor's comments and are able to move the conversation on.

Opportunities for IT

The children could use a word processor to write their letter of thanks. Older or more able children could be shown how to lay out the letter, placing the address in the correct position, using the right justification command, and using the centring command (if required) for the 'Yours faithfully' line.

Display ideas

Make a class visitors' book. Let the children draw or paint portraits of the visitors, writing out their names beneath the pictures. They might turn it into a scrapbook, asking the

Discuss with the children how they think they might make the visitor welcome in school: meet them at the front door, show them where the headteacher's room/staff room is, ask if they would like to hang up their coat, show the way to your classroom.

Give a badge to each child and ask them to write their name on it, so that the visitor will know who they are. Make a WELCOME TO OUR SCHOOL banner, getting the children to fill in the letter outlines with paint or felt-tipped pen.

Help the children to write welcoming notes to their visitors. These should include a map showing how to get to the school. Ask the children to draw portraits (with names) of the people who make up the school community: Mrs Green the kitchen supervisor, Mrs Thompson the head teacher, Mr Hinksman the caretaker and so on. On the day of the visit, ask these people to wear name badges, all of which should have been made and labelled by the children.

Discuss with the children what things make them proud of the school and what they would not want the visitor to know/see. Why? Make two lists, *Good* and *Not So Good*. (What can they do about the latter? Pick up litter? Tidy the school garden?)

Choose two children to station themselves near the front door, ready to meet the visitor. The children may first take the visitor to meet the headteacher. Then they can show her or him to their classroom, perhaps pointing out the library and/or the assembly hall on the way. Ask them to show the

SPEAKING AND
LISTENING

guests if they can leave a memento of their visit. This might take the form of a poem, a book jacket, a seed packet and so on. These items can be pasted onto backing paper on the wall, beside the visitor's portrait.

Other aspects of the English PoS covered
Reading – 1d.
Writing – 1a, c; 2a, b, e.

THE FACE IN THE MIRROR

To give children the opportunity to organise and present information about what they see.

†† *Whole class or group.*

🕐 *20 minutes.*

Key background information
It is important that children learn to expand their powers of description. This activity helps children to explore the language used to describe facial characteristics, hair and so on. It requires you to be ready with the next open question, so that the children are pressed into expanding their answers – to go, for example, from *'I see my face.'* to *'I see a boy's face. He has freckles on his nose.'* It can be used as a regular activity, so that every child has an opportunity both to pose questions and to answer them.

Preparation
This activity needs to be supervised carefully in order to prevent any unkind behaviour.

Figure 4

Resources needed
A hand mirror which can be passed from one child to the next; or better still, a set of small safety mirrors, one for each child in the group. One copy per child of photocopiable sheet 136.

What to do
Ask the children to sit in a semicircle. Show them a mirror. Look at the way it reflects light. Let them see you look into the mirror and ask them to tell you what they think you will see in it. Encourage them to expand on the simple answer *'Your face!'*

Ask the children to help you describe the face you are looking at, so that they can begin to build up a portrait in words. Encourage description: not just *'hair'*, but *'curly hair'*,

'long hair', *'tousled hair'*. Help the children to explore details of what you look like, for example, *'freckles on your cheeks'*, *'pink lipstick'*, *'long shiny earrings'* and so on.

Now suggest that one child looks in the mirror for a moment. You should ask the first question, *'What do you see?'* If the answer is simply *'My face'*, ask another question, for example, *'Is it a girl's face or a boy's face?'* This should elicit a fuller reply, such as *'I see a girl's face.'* Ask *'What does her hair look like?'* Encourage the child to answer in terms of colour, style and so on, for example: *'My/Her hair is black and straight. I have/She has a red hair-band.'*

Get each child to frame three questions to ask another member of the group, for example: *'What colour eyes can you see?' 'What kind of hair can you see?' 'How many teeth can you see?'* The children should be encouraged to give factual answers, always beginning, *'I can see...'*

This kind of question and answer session, with its formula answers, helps children to organise their thoughts into coherent sentences. It provides some of the 'tools' with which to expand description beyond simple two- or three-word answers.

After looking at themselves in the mirror, the children should draw and colour self-portraits inside the mirror frame on photocopiable sheet 136. After they have done this, jumble up the sheets, giving a 'portrait' to each child. Ask them to describe the face they see – looking not at the 'sitter', but only at the drawing.

Suggestion(s) for extension
Suggest that each child look over his or her shoulder into a mirror. Ask them to describe what they see. By asking probing questions, encourage them to notice and describe, for example, that a clock *'has the numbers back to front'*, that they can see the classroom charts with colour names, days of the week and so on, *'looking the wrong way round'*.

A further extension with a group of able children is to make up a story which is set in the land of mirrors, where everything is swapped from left to right. *Through the Magic Mirror* by Anthony Browne (Picture Puffins, 1995) could be a useful starting point for thinking about how mirrors change what we see.

Suggestion(s) for support
Put a small group of children in twos, pairing an able child with a less able one. Using a mirror between two, encourage

The face in the mirror

Name _____

Date _____

them to think of colour words to describe eyes and hair. Ask them to make up simple descriptive sentences, using some of the colour words they have thought of, for example: *'I can see a boy with blue eyes and brown hair.' 'I can see a girl with grey eyes and blonde hair.'*

Assessment opportunities

Note the children's ability to use descriptive words and to understand what they mean. Note whether they have difficulty in going beyond the simple two- or three-word answers.

Opportunities for IT

The children could use an art package to draw their own self-portrait from the mirror image. They could focus on getting the correct colours for hair and eyes. They may need to be shown how to mix colours that are not immediately available from the palette provided. They could add their names using the text facilities of the art package.

Display ideas

Make a large floor-sized 'photograph album' in which the children can stick self-portraits, each with the child's name printed beneath.

Use the self-portraits from the photocopiable sheets cut out and pasted up collage-style on a foil backing, to make a framed group. (See Figure 4.) Label it *What the mirror saw.*

Other aspects of the English PoS covered

Reading – 1d.

Writing – 1b, c; 2a, b.

Reference to photocopiable sheet

The children can use photocopiable sheet 136 to draw or paint their own self-portraits, based on looking in a mirror. The completed sheets are then passed on to other children, who describe what is drawn there. This links to discussion of mirror-images and portraits.

YOU WON'T BELIEVE THIS!

To give children practice in listening to and repeating an unusual message.

†† *Groups of six to eight children.*

🕐 *20 minutes.*

Previous skills/knowledge needed

Some experience of informal weighing: *The brick feels heavier than the pencil. The feather feels lighter than my reading book,* and so on.

Preparation

Wrap an empty rectangular box in coloured paper, so that it looks like an exciting present.

Resources needed

An empty box (as above), a flip chart or whiteboard.

What to do

Work with one group at a time, letting them handle the parcel. Tell them that this is a guessing game; but instead of guessing what the box might contain, ask the children to suggest things that cannot possibly be inside!

SPEAKING AND
LISTENING

It is so light that the children will deduce immediately that there are no ice skates or bricks inside, for example. *It cannot be a football because it is the wrong shape. It cannot be a kite, it is too small.* Take time to allow the children to speculate, concentrating on what is *not* there.

Now begin to float the idea of something fantastic. Would a fallen star be too heavy? What about moonshine? Could the parcel contain a breath of wind? Encourage the children to examine more fantastic ideas of their own.

Once they have settled on an idea, *a moonbeam* for example, talk about how it got into the parcel, who is to receive it, who it is from.

Now the children must go to another group with their fantastic story. They should show them the parcel, tell them to take great care of it because inside – now they should whisper – *'Inside, you won't believe it, is a silver moonbeam. It is supposed to have come from the North Wind one winter night. He is sending it to his cousin, the Princess of the Mountains because there has been a power cut in her castle and she has no light to read by.'*

(It is useful to listen to the message as the children in the first group tell it, scribing it on the whiteboard out of sight. Emphasise how secret the message is.)

The children should only tell their message once. Then the group who have just received the message should pass it on to the next group, Chinese whispers fashion. When it gets to the last group, they should finally pass it on to you. Scribe what they tell you on the flip chart or whiteboard and read it with the children.

Read the first message over to the children and contrast what was said then with the most recent message. Has the message changed? If so, in what ways? Let the first group tell the others how accurate or otherwise the final message is.

This activity demands that the children speak clearly and listen carefully, and the children find it a lot of fun. The other groups who are eager to have an opportunity to devise another 'magic message' can either use the same parcel or use some more empty boxes of different shapes which you have made for them. The latter will encourage more independent thinking.

Ask the children to draw a box and then make a bright pattern on its outside, like exciting-looking wrapping paper. Suggest that the children work with a partner, using a question-and-answer dialogue to guess what present might be concealed in the box. Child A asks a question, for example: *Is it a football?* (in the rectangular box). Child B says: *No. Try again,* and so on.

Suggestion(s) for extension

A group of more able children could make up more stories in the oral tradition by suggesting: what might have happened to an unusual stone to make it into a particular shape, how a poppy came to be painted red, what is hidden inside a shell. Each group passes their story to the next, and so on.

Suggestion(s) for support

Help children to think of fantastic ideas for the parcel by prompting them with questions: *'Do you think there is a kite inside the parcel?' 'No, there can't be a kite.' 'How do you know that?' 'The parcel is too small/isn't the correct shape.' 'Can you think of another toy that is too big/too round/too heavy to be inside this parcel?'*

Some children may find it easier to work with a partner's help.

Assessment opportunities

Note the children who listen attentively to the passed-on message and can pass it on accurately, and those who change the information given or do not know what to say. Find out whether they have simply 'switched off', did not hear correctly or do not remember.

Display ideas

Make a painted collage with two matching rectangular decorated boxes in the middle. Show a number of toys, foods, shooting out of one. Scribe question labels: *'Is it a football?' 'Is it a frisbee?' 'Is it a cauliflower?'* Show fantastic things shooting out of the other box, scribing *'Is it a moonbeam?' 'Is it a monster?' 'Is it a dragon?'* and so on. Label the frieze *'You won't believe this!'* (See illustration above.)

Other aspects of the English PoS covered

Writing – 1b, c.

SPEAKING AND LISTENING

Explaining and understanding

In our everyday lives, there are many occasions on which we must be able to explain a process or a situation with clarity using appropriate and precise language. This section is designed to give children practice in understanding and explaining processes with which they may be initially unfamiliar. They are expected to use instructive descriptive language to explain how things work and to demonstrate a new process.

The children are also asked to explore pictures and paintings with questioning eyes. In an attempt to understand what is going on inside the pictures, they have to frame appropriate questions and seek out imaginative answers. In the activity 'An artist's ear', the children have to use clear descriptive language, as well as listening and responding to instructions.

This chapter encourages the children's accurate use of the language of the senses, especially those of touch and hearing. It also gives practice in expressing the language of colour. Through the above activities, not only are the children's speaking skills developed and refined, but they are encouraged to listen and respond appropriately to instruction and explanation.

SPEAKING AND
LISTENING

DETECTIVES

To encourage children's use of descriptive language, with particular reference to their sense of touch.

†† *Whole class.*

🕐 *20 minutes.*

Key background information

This activity is intended to stimulate the children's interest in and knowledge of 'touch words', so it is essential to insist that the children work 'in secret', giving clues to the feel of the object, but not giving away its identity. Tell them they have to help each other become detectives!

Preparation

The activity 'Surprise, surprise' could be used to introduce the idea of touching and describing unseen objects. Cut two holes, big enough for a child's hand to go through, in either side of a cardboard box (a shoebox is ideal). (See Figure 1.)

Figure 1

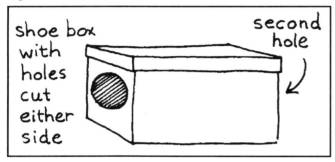

shoe box with holes cut either side

second hole

Resources needed

A box (as above); a selection of differently-textured objects, such as a piece of bubble wrap, a pineapple, a ball of wool, a toothbrush, a mirror; one copy per child of photocopiable sheet 137.

What to do

Sit the children around you in the book corner. Produce the box with, for example, an orange hidden inside. Tell them that you are going to play a guessing game. Although it is simply the old 'touch box' routine, give it a new twist by suggesting that the children are to be detectives. They have to guess what is hidden in the box just from clues which describe, not what it is, but how it feels.

Start the game off, showing how it is played. Put your hand into the box and give the first 'touch' clue: *It feels like a ball.* Encourage the children to ask questions so that it develops into a question and answer session. They may ask, *Can you play with it?* After answering that you can not play with it, give another touch clue: *I can feel it rolling around the box. There is a little round piece like a button on the top.* Go on in this fashion until the children have done their detective work and they ask, *Can you eat it?*

To begin with, you may need to help the children with the kind of question to ask; but they soon understand what is required.

Now it is the turn of the children. Allow a child to choose one of the objects in secret. He or she should hide it in the box, put their hands through the hole and tell the others what the hidden object feels like.

What they may find difficult at first is *not* saying what the object is, but simply giving touch clues. Encourage them to explore the ideas of shape, relative size and texture.

When they are asked *What does it feel like?* do not accept just *smooth*, but encourage them to pursue the idea. *Smooth as ...?* It can be smooth as ice-cream, as a mirror, as a black cat's coat, as velvet.

Try to give everybody a turn, perhaps not the first time round, but on some other occasion.

After working through a number of touch words, turn the activity around and get the children to match up the touch words on photocopiable sheet 137 with things that feel *shiny, rough, hairy* and so on. Discuss the children's ideas and ask them to draw three pictures in each set – for example, under *shiny* they might draw a mirror, a coin and a windowpane.

Suggestion(s) for extension

Let the children try this activity from a different angle. Ask a group of about five children to explore with their fingers, in secret, a grapefruit, a pencil or a shell, for example, either using the touch box or simply feeling without looking. They should each find one thing to say about how it feels. They then return to the main group to give their five touch clues. As soon as those in the audience think they can guess the object's identity they can raise their hands, but must not call

SPEAKING AND LISTENING

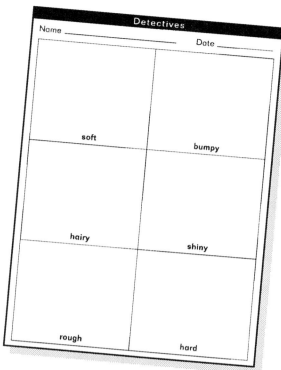

out. The children in the group of five should choose someone to answer, going from one member of the audience to another until the object is correctly guessed. Then another group takes over.

Suggestion(s) for support

If there are children who find it difficult to find the vocabulary for this activity, help them by offering leading questions: *Is it rough or smooth? Is it round like a ball or round like a plate?* Get them to answer using the appropriate words back to you: *Yes, it is smooth. It feels round like a ball.*

Assessment opportunities

Give the children a selection of objects similar to those already used (for example: a ball of string, a hairbrush, a marble, a peach) and ask them to suggest ways of describing the feel of these new objects. Encourage them to use touch words and images with which they have already become familiar. They might say, *The peach is round like the moon and feels as fuzzy as a new tennis ball.*

Opportunities for IT

Children who are writing independently could use a word processor to write their own 'What am I?' riddle. They may be able to add a picture, drawn with an art package, to their writing. The picture could be hidden under a flap.

Display ideas

Make a textured 'quilt' with off-cuts of different materials. Glue scraps of *soft, shiny, bubbly, rough* and *hairy* materials on to a quartered background with the appropriate touch

word displayed above them. On the display table below, lay out a selection of objects, again divided into sets by touch, for example: shells, stones, a brick, a brass bell.

Other aspects of the English PoS covered
Reading – 2b.

Reference to photocopiable sheet
The children use the touch sets on photocopiable sheet 137 to draw three objects which fit into each word column.

HERE IS WHAT YOU DO

To help children to listen to and pass on instructions accurately.

†† *Two groups of five or six children.*

🕐 *30 minutes.*

Previous skills/knowledge needed

It is useful, but not strictly necessary, for the children already to understand the class rules for working with paint, for example: wearing protective aprons/painting shirts, how to clean used brushes.

Key background knowledge

This activity depends on the children watching and listening to the demonstration of a new art technique, so it is essential that you are completely familiar with the process. Because you have to concentrate on one group who will be watching your demonstration, you will need to organise a different task to interest the rest of the class.

Preparation

Cover the painting area with old newspapers.

Resources needed

Old newspapers, good quality A4 paper, thick poster paint, thick brushes, painting aprons.

What to do

Work with one group, demonstrating how to make blob mirror-pattern pictures. Show the materials required: A4 paper, thick poster paint, clean thick brushes. Stress the importance of covering the tables in newspaper and wearing painting aprons. Set out the pots of paint and the brushes, one pot of paint and one brush for each member of the group.

Demonstrate folding the A4 paper down the middle and then opening it out. Having laid it down on the newspaper, put thick blobs of poster paint on the right-hand half of the page, trying to keep them near the middle crease. Next fold the paper over, creasing the middle and pressing down hard. Show how it makes a mirror pattern when it is opened out. Let the first group have a go for themselves.

71

Once they have tidied up, the first group should take on the teacher's role. They should work with a second group, first showing the materials required, then demonstrating, step-by-step, how to make the mirror patterns. Now they should leave the second group to assemble the materials they need and to follow their instructions for making blob mirror patterns. This activity requires that the children be able, not only to demonstrate, but to talk the others through the process.

Ask the children to look carefully at the other children's finished work. Suggest that they comment on the blob patterns, talking about what they think they represent – for example, *Anita's pattern looks like a mountain with fire coming out the top. Kwok's pattern looks like two dragons fighting. No, I think it's more like two ships on a stormy sea*, and so on. Encourage constructive and imaginative discussion.

When everyone has finished, bring the two groups together to go over the process. If the second group had a problem, let them work out why. Let them try to assess the clarity of the instructions and show where, for example, a step was left out.

Suggestion(s) for extension
Ask the children in either the first or second group to pass on instructions for making mirror patterns to another group – or better still, to children in another class – without a demonstration, simply by talking the process through.

Suggestion(s) for support
Children who need support can work in two pairs, one pair demonstrating and talking, the other pair watching and listening. This way there are fewer distractions and each of

Figure 3

the four children has the opportunity to feel he or she is taking part; they will not feel dominated by more confident children.

Assessment opportunities
Watch and listen to the way in which the second group tackles the activity:
▲ Have they assembled all the required materials?
▲ Has the first group explained the process accurately?
▲ Has the second group listened carefully?
▲ Can every member of the second group carry out the instructions?
▲ Have all the children thought about and commented on what the blob patterns look like?

Figure 2

Opportunities for IT
The children could use a word processor to create a list of instructions for making the mirror patterns. They could print this out in a large font style to go alongside the display of patterns produced. Once they have created the instructions, the children could test them out with another child or another class.

Display ideas
Turn the mirror patterns into birthday cards (see Figure 2). Print *Happy Birthday* on the front in bubble-writing. A card shop could be set up in the classroom, where children can sell and buy the cards as part of a maths activity.

Get the children to make the patterns into 'mirror monsters' by adding teeth or hair and filling in fierce eyes with a different colour of paint. Then they can cut the monsters out and make a collage-style gallery of monsters.

Other aspects of the English PoS covered
Reading – 1c; 2b.
Writing – 1c; 2e.

Performance ideas
The children can make large-size blob 'mirror-monsters', big enough to be made into masks. Add ties made from strings or laces, or tape an old ruler on the underside as a handle (see Figure 3), and make up a monster play.

HOW DOES IT WORK?

To help the children explain how a natural process (or a machine) works.

†† *Groups of about eight to ten children under supervision.*

🕑 *20 minutes.*

⚠ *Candles and matches must be lit only by the teacher, with the children being supervised and kept well away from flames.*

Previous skills/knowledge needed
An ability to listen with understanding.

Key background knowledge
This activity is based on the simple scientific principle that a candle needs air to burn. **Note**: although it is suggested that this activity be built around candles and their need for air, another simple scientific procedure could be used instead. The passing on of accurate explanations is the important feature of this activity. If, for safety reasons, you do not want to use a candle in the classroom, try an experiment with wet and dry kitchen sponges showing how a sponge absorbs water, but keeps its shape. Show what happens when you weigh the two sponges. If you have special knowledge of, for example, how a clock works or the inner workings of a vacuum cleaner, be prepared to share this with some of the children so that they, in turn, can pass it on to others.

Preparation
Make sure that the first group *sits* round a table and that neither candles nor matches are left unattended.

Resources needed
Candle, glass jam jar, safety matches (in your control at all times) *or* two matching kitchen sponges, pan scales, a bowl of water. One copy per child of the photocopiable summative assessment sheet on page 138 (if required).

What to do
Work with one group. Talk with the children about where and when we use candles: *festivals – Hannukah, Diwali; birthday cakes; Christingle service; in church; when we have*

a power cut. Discuss with the children the dangers of lighted candles, that they can burn clothes, hair and skin.

Ask children to say how we light a candle. Show the box of matches and reiterate the safety message. Light the candle and watch the flame. Is it a steady light? Blow gently on the flame and watch it dance. Now ask the children if they can guess what will happen to the candle if you cover it with the jam jar. Accept their guesses, then put the jar over the candle and watch what happens. Why do they think the flame went out? Establish that lack of air snuffed out the flame.

Take time to talk about other things that need air, for example, animals and humans. Then suggest that they explain to another group about the flame needing air. Do they need to ask any more questions before they begin?

Gather the second group around the table and get the first group of children to take over. Tell them that you will light the candle when they are ready. Encourage them to talk about how and when candles are used, the need for safety and so on.

Light the candle when the children ask and encourage them to go through the same procedure as you did earlier. Listen to their explanations. Can they establish that the candle needs air to burn?

Encourage members of the second group to ask questions of the first. Listen to their answers and explanations. Try to find out whether the second group understands what the first is trying to explain.

Get all the children together and ask the two groups who have been working with the candles to explain what they were doing and what they found out to the rest of the class.

In a further session, try out other simple experiments with different groups, again encouraging detailed explanations of what is happening and why.

Suggestion(s) for extension
Suggest that more able children bring something in from home, for example, a mechanical toy, so that they can demonstrate it and explain to the others how it works (if they can do this without taking it apart).

Suggestion(s) for support
Children who are experiencing difficulty should work in a small group with a supportive adult. They should be encouraged to ask questions and repeat the explanations.

SPEAKING AND LISTENING

Assessment opportunities

This activity can be used for summative assessment, and photocopiable sheet 138 is provided for this purpose. Listen to the language of the children's explanations. Can they follow through the process step-by-step? Can the listeners interpret the explanations correctly and ask relevant questions?

Figure 4

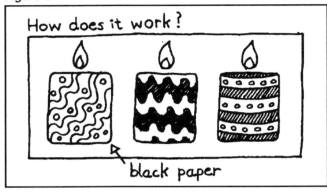

Display ideas

Using wax crayons or a sharpened candle-end, the children can make wax resist patterns (painted over with thin poster paint) on fat candle shapes. Use foil for the 'flames'. Mount the decorated 'candles' on a wall display (see Figure 4).

They could also make wax rubbings of bark or coin patterns and then brush over them with thinly mixed paint.

Reference to photocopiable sheet

Photocopiable sheet 138 is provided for summative assessment of the children's skills in explaining and understanding, based on this activity.

MAKING CORNER CARDS

To help children to listen to instructions, carry them out and explain the process in fluent, clear language.

†† *Groups of six.*

🕑 *20 minutes.*

Previous skills/knowledge needed

The children should be capable of folding, sticking and cutting card.

Key background information

This activity is based on card-making. Decide which festival or special day is the most appropriate one to celebrate: Mother's Day, Easter, Diwali, Christmas – or you could make a collection of birthday cards for the classroom shop.

The activity falls into several sessions: a learning session for the first group, who then pass on what they have learned to the next group and so on, until everyone has had the opportunity to make a card. Much depends on the children's ability to listen to instructions with concentration and understanding.

Preparation

Set out an activity table with the necessary materials, making sure that the working groups are wearing protective shirts or aprons. Cover the activity table with old newspapers before the children start work.

Resources needed

Old newspapers, fine card or sugar paper cut into squares (approximately 300mm x 300mm), strips of card (for the bookmarks), felt-tipped pens, adhesive or paste, rounded scissors, paper doilies, discarded seed packets, a flip chart.

What to do

Choose a group to start the activity off. Show them how to fold the sugar paper in four. Stand the card up on the folded edge, so that the open sides are at the top. Fold down the top corner, as shown in Figure 5. Let the children choose their greeting, *Happy birthday, Happy Easter, Happy Mother's Day* or whatever is most appropriate. Scribe the words on the flip chart and get the children to copy them in felt-tipped pen.

Suggest to the children that they edge the turned-over corners with a scrap of doily, then encourage them to decorate the card in their own way; with felt-tipped pen illustrations or by cutting and sticking flowers from the seed packets. They finish by making a decorated bookmark and slipping it into the corner pocket.

Encourage the children in this group to go over, step-by-step, the procedure for making the cards. Stress that they are going to teach the others how to do it, so they must be quite sure of the process. Make sure that their explanations

SPEAKING AND LISTENING

are accurate and that they can express themselves with clarity.

When the second group is ready (they should meanwhile have been engaged in a different activity), the children in the first group take on the role of teachers. They should lay out the necessary materials. Then they must explain how to fold the card, turn down the corners and stand it on the folded edge.

They can then suggest ways of decorating the card and the bookmark, reminding everyone that they should copy the greeting from the flip chart.

Now this group, in turn, prepares the table for another group and takes over the role of explaining the process. (They should do this verbally, without demonstrating.) Listen to the children's explanations and be available to help out if they get stuck, but try to remain in the background.

Finish off this activity by bringing all the children together to admire their work and to talk through it with them.

Figure 5

Suggestion(s) for extension
More able children can use their expertise by explaining to a group in another classroom how to make a corner card. This means that they will be entirely on their own and cannot turn to you for support.

A further extension is to have children in this group explain a different process for card-making. This could be a process that they have learned from a book.

Suggestion(s) for support
Children who need support may need to work on a one-to-one basis and could explain the card-making process to a co-operative adult.

Assessment opportunities
Listen to the children working. Are their explanations clear and concise? Do those who are 'learners' have enough accurate information to work through the process in a logical fashion? Does it require your intervention?

Display ideas
The children could make a card shop with posters, price tickets and labels. They might make fancy wrapping paper to 'sell' along with their cards.

Other aspects of the English PoS covered
Reading – 1c; 2b.
Writing – 1c; 2b, e.

WHAT'S HAPPENING?

To give practice in using dialogue to make deductions and to speculate.

†† *Whole class, then working in pairs.*

🕑 *30 minutes, including paired activity.*

Previous skills/knowledge needed
Children should have some experience of talking about illustrations in picture books.

Key background information
It is best to begin this activity by introducing the concept of situation speculation to the whole class. Suggest that they are going to make 'stories from pictures' and help them to look for clues about what is happening/has happened/will happen next from details in the picture.

Resources needed
A number of detailed pictures, large enough to be seen easily by all the children, showing relatively complex situations (patients waiting in the casualty area of a hospital with nurses, porters, ambulance workers rushing around; lots of activity in the control section of a space rocket; passengers checking in at an airport, people meeting one another, one lost child). Also see photocopiable pages 139 and 140, which can be used as a basis for story-making by pairs of children or enlarged for whole-class work. Along with newspaper colour supplements, useful sources for pictures include the magazines *Child Education* and *Junior Education* (Scholastic), which often have large, 'busy' posters in the project sections.

What to do
Group the children in the story corner and ask them to look closely at one of the pictures. Get them to consider what is going on in the picture, taking a minute or two to look and think in silence. Then, using open questioning, ask them to

speculate about where the scene is taking place, who the people are, what might have happened immediately before the moment shown, what might happen next.

Give the children time to explore the picture again so they can suggest new ideas and find more details to substantiate their own speculations. Work together to build up a story around the principal characters.

Divide the group into pairs with a picture between them. Through dialogue with a partner, get the children to work out what has happened; is happening; is going to happen; where it is taking place; who the main characters are and why they are there.

Give the children five minutes or so to come up with a story about their picture. Then ask them to share it with the rest of the class.

After discussing the story-making technique with the whole class, this task can be confined to one group at one session. Later, children in other groups can take their turn. This will enhance the involvement of the children, as well as the effectiveness of teaching.

important characters in the scene, asking subsequent direct questions – for example, point to the ambulance: *Why has it stopped, do you think? (Because there's been an accident.) How do you think the accident happened? (The car bumped into a boy on his bike.) What makes you think that? (The bike is on the road and the boy is sitting holding his head.) What about the car? Perhaps the driver saw the boy fall off and has stopped to help. What do you think?* and so on. Encourage discussion, then help the group to build their story piece by piece, making further deductions as they go along.

Assessment opportunities

This activity offers excellent opportunities to examine informally the children's ability to use the language of deduction and speculation, *What do you think? What if ...? What next?*

Opportunities for IT

Still working in their groups, the children could write their story using a word processor or simple desk-top publishing package. If the story is split into three parts, each pair could write one section. A template could be set up in advance to make the format easier to handle. The children could also use an art package to add their own illustrations to the story.

Display ideas

Make a three-part wall frieze, *Past, Present and Future,* based on the original picture, using a collage technique so that all the children can make a contribution. Use the children's own version of the picture as the middle part *(Present),* the section on the left should be what has happened *(Past)* and the

Suggestion(s) for extension

Suggest that the children in one group look for a 'busy' picture in a book from the school/class library. Ask them to make up a story in the same way as above, then pass the picture to another group. This second group should also devise a story from the same picture. Both groups should work in secret. Get the class together to hear both stories. Compare the stories and discuss the differences, if any. Ask the listeners which story they consider to be more interesting – and why.

Suggestion(s) for support

If some children find it difficult to make deductions about what is happening in the picture, work with them in a small group of about five or six. Encourage them to point out

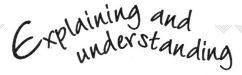

section on the right what is going to happen next *(Future)*. All three pictures should feature the same characters in the same setting.

Other aspects of the English PoS covered
Reading – 1b, 2c.
Writing – 3a.

Reference to photocopiable sheets
The children could use photocopiable sheets 139 and 140 as a basis for the paired discussion (see 'What to do'), or the sheets could be enlarged for work with the whole class. Ask the children to talk about the main characters, the family groups and so on. Suggest that they think about the people who work in each location. What might they be saying? What other sounds might be heard? Get the children to speculate about what the children/adults in the pictures are doing, how they feel, why they are there.

Performance ideas
The three-part story which the children have developed from the original picture can be used to create a performance. Use minimal props: hats, painted and cut-out 'tools', simple masks and so on.

WHAT'S THAT SOUND?

To develop children's use of descriptive language with particular reference to sound. To encourage listening skills.

†† *Whole class, then working in pairs, (as many as you have cassette players and headsets for).*

⏱ *10 minutes.*

Previous skills/knowledge needed
The children should be familiar with using a cassette player.

Key background information
This activity develops both listening and language skills. You should be ready to encourage the children to concentrate on, not what is making the sound they hear, but a description of what it is like. Try to make this clear to the children in your introduction to the activity.

If you don't have enough cassette players and headsets, use what you have and make this an ongoing activity, using the cassette players as and when they become available.

Preparation
Make a cassette recording of some familiar sounds: a kettle boiling, a door slamming, a bee buzzing, children in the playground, a car alarm. (There are cassettes available commercially with a range of these sounds. Try your local teachers' centre loan service.)

Resources needed
A cassette recording of familiar sounds (as above), cassette players and headsets for the children working in pairs, a flip chart or whiteboard.

What to do
Have the children sit where they can hear the cassette player easily. Ask them to close their eyes and listen to the sounds on the tape. Play, for example, a snatch of bird song. Ask the children to put their hands up to indicate if they know what the sound is. When most of the hands are in the air, tell the children to open their eyes again.

Ask if anyone can describe, not what was making the noise they heard, but what it sounds like. This tests the

children's skills in both listening and language. For example:
▲ It sounds like a song.
▲ It sounds like tweeting.
▲ It has a soft sound.
▲ It sounds like it's in the morning.

Let the children decide what descriptions seem best. Scribe these ideas on the flip chart or whiteboard.

Now divide some of the children into pairs, and give each pair a cassette player and headset. One child should listen to the sounds on the headset, then describe what he hears. The other child should guess what it is just from her partner's description.

Suggestion(s) for extension
Get the children to listen to snatches of different kinds of instrumental music: jazz, classical and pop. Encourage them

77

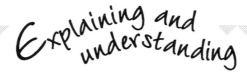

to think about the sounds they have heard and to express their ideas in words. What do the instruments, melody, rhythm sound like?

Suggestion(s) for support

To help children who find this activity difficult, work with small groups of three or four, taking them step by step through the procedure.

Assessment opportunities

Note any children who have difficulty in hearing sounds on tape. Check whether these children are in need of a hearing test. For the rest, listen for interesting descriptive language and note those who need more practice.

Opportunities for IT

The children's use of a cassette player to record their own descriptions involves them in controlling an everyday device, and should be seen as a part of their IT experience.

Display ideas

The children can paint large pictures of what makes actual sounds such as: birds, a car or a kettle. Scribe or have the children copy their oral descriptions of the sounds inset into bubble or cloud formation, then paste these around the main picture. (See illustration below.)

Other aspects of the English PoS covered

Reading – 1c; 2b.
Writing – 1a, b, c.

Performance ideas

The children can make up riddles from their descriptions, recording them on tape. The answers can take the form of the sound itself played on tape. This makes an interesting assembly presentation for a topic on the senses.

WHY? WHY? WHY?

To give children practice in asking questions and thinking of logical (but fantastic) answers.

†† *Whole class, then working in pairs.*

🕐 *20 minutes.*

Previous skills/knowledge needed

Children who have a wide experience of the traditional fairy story culture respond well to the imaginative demands of this activity.

Key background information

This activity requires imagination on behalf of both teacher and children. Begin from a fairly mundane basis, perhaps a photograph, or better still, a painting, showing an everyday scene. (There is usually more scope for the imagination in a painting, because an artist has already interpreted a scene and he or she will often leave the work open to further interpretation.) You will find that the children thrive on this fantasy approach, vying with each other to be ever more outlandish, once the idea has been established.

Preparation

Think up your own possible replies to the *Why? Why? Why?* questions for the first picture you select.

Resources needed

A set of pictures, photographs, or paintings in which a child or an animal is involved in an active way, for example: a child jumping on a sand castle, a cat at the top of a tree, a child creeping downstairs in the dark. One copy per pair of photocopiable sheet 141, or an enlarged copy for the whole class.

What to do

To help stimulate the imagination required for this activity, first gather the children in the story corner and show them a picture. Tell them that they are going to play a guessing game. They must think up 'why?' questions, for example: Why is the cat up the tree? Because the dog chased her. Why? Because the cat tried to take his dinner. Why? Because she was hungry. Why? Because she was out all night. Why? (Now move from realistic answers to fantastic ones.) Because she wanted to count the stars.

Give practice in imaginative replies, still working from the first picture. Start again and look for different ideas: Why is the cat up the tree? Because she wanted to catch the birds/ Because she wanted to get closer to the sun/Because she liked the view. Pursue each of these answers to see where it can lead, and observe how the children become more

SPEAKING AND LISTENING

simple picture. Ask no more than three 'why' questions and try, with your own suggestions, to lead them from the purely factual towards an imaginative idea. There are some children who are frightened of moving from the realm of fact and feel that they need licence to do so.

Assessment opportunities
Note how well children are able to talk in imaginative language and can support their ideas with reference to what is happening in the picture.

Display ideas
Some of the stories created can be made into cartoon-type wall displays, using an A3 sheet for each episode. Pin the frieze above a table display which shows picture story-books standing open. Use drapes made from net with trailing ribbons. Add shells, bare branches painted silver, 'cobwebs' made from string and beaded with sequins, mirrors and so on, creating an impression of pure fantasy. (See illustration above.)

With independent writers, such fantasy stories are ideal for putting into zigzag story-book format. Stand these open among the objects on the table display.

Other aspects of the English PoS covered
Reading – 1b, c.
Writing – 1b; 2a.

Reference to photocopiable sheet
The pictures on photocopiable sheet 141 are meant to stimulate discussion at a variable level of practicality or imagination.

involved and imaginative as the activity proceeds.

Once the children understand what is wanted of them, they can play the 'Why? Why? Why?' game for themselves. Divide the children into pairs. Give one of the partners a picture. The other has to ask the questions, each of which must begin with the word Why? The first child makes up a fantastic story to go with the picture, the more outrageous the better!

The second child records the number of answers the first child can manage before he has to give up. They can change places. It could be made into a group game where the player with the greatest number of answers wins.

Use photocopiable sheet 141 either for paired discussion or (enlarged) for the whole-class work. Encourage the children to work from factual probabilities – The child is on a school visit to a castle. The firefighter is trying to rescue the cat. – to fantastic ideas, for example: The child is off to see if 'Jack and the Beanstalk' is a true story. The firefighter wants to be a spaceman and is getting ready to take his cat on a moonwalk.

Suggestion(s) for extension
Use the same technique to make up a story to go with an object, for example, a well-polished stone. This time the children can ask questions beginning with, Where? Why? When? What? Who? and How?

Where was the stone found? On a far-off island. How did it get there? It was washed up by the tide. When did it happen? Last full moon. And so on.

Suggestion(s) for support
Look out for the one or two children who can not get into the game. Often they are the least confident members of the group. Put them together and show them a

Performance ideas

Make the stories that the children have created from their *Why?* questions into short plays or mimes to be performed in front of another class, perhaps as an assembly item.

AN ARTIST'S EAR

To develop children's skills of accurate description, and listening and responding to such description.

†† *Whole class or large individual groups for the introduction, pairs for the activity.*

🕐 *30 minutes.*

Previous skills/knowledge needed

Experience in discussing the content of illustrations in picture books (see activity 'What's happening?' on page 75).

Key background information

This activity is a version of the old party game *Blind Man's Buff*. The process consists of looking carefully and in detail at a picture, describing it (content, colours, shapes) accurately to someone who has not seen it. That person then has to draw her or his version of the picture from the oral description alone.

Preparation

You may wish to organise the children into pairs, so that they know who their partners are, before you introduce the activity. Build a screen between the partners (up-ended hardback books will do).

Resources needed

As many simple pictures or photographs as there are pairs of children involved, paper, coloured pencils or felt-tipped pens, pencils, a flip chart or whiteboard.

What to do

You may wish to explain the process either to a whole class or to a group, so gather the children around you and ask if they know how to play *Blind Man's Buff*. Remind them that one person has to guess a friend's identity while being blindfolded.

Take one of the pictures and ask the children to describe what they can see in it. For example, if it is a picture of an apple and a vase of flowers on a table ask the children first to name the main parts (flowers, apple, tablecloth). Then ask about colours, if the apple is whole or cut up, if it is behind or in front of the flowers and so on. Encourage accurate description.

Let the children choose another picture, one which you have not seen, and to keep it hidden from you. Ask them to describe it in a similar way. Ask them questions that will help to provide accuracy. *How many windows in the house? What colour is the door? Is it a sunny day?* and so on. From their description, draw your version of the picture on the whiteboard.

This activity arouses a great deal of interesting comment! Compare the two versions. *How are they different? What makes them different? What about differences in colour, in shapes, in the way things are placed on the page?* Use this as a briefing session to help children to understand the need for accurate description.

Divide the group into their pairs and explain that one child in each pair should describe a picture, the other draw from the oral description only. Sometimes those children who are taking the part of the artist will be too concerned 'to get it right', but reassure them that the end result does not matter too much. (Remind them of your own efforts – see above.)

Put up a screen between the partners, give one a picture, the other paper and coloured pencils. Encourage the child with the picture to describe what is in it, the main colours, weather, shapes and so on. The 'artist' can ask a few questions to get a better idea of what to draw. Give them five to ten minutes to complete the activity; then they should change places and pictures.

Take time to compare the original pictures with the new versions. Try to keep this session light and enjoyable, but ask what might have been said to make the description clearer. Concentrate on the vocabulary of colour: *light green, minty green, forest green*; of comparison: *taller than the trees, smaller than the flowers*; of place: *under the branches, on top of the gate, above the roof* and so on, consciously trying to extend and develop the children's command of descriptive

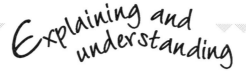

language. Emphasise, too, the need for the 'artists' to listen carefully.

Suggestion(s) for extension

Children can work in threes so that one child gets into an unusual position, for example on hands and one foot, while the second child describes this position to the third one who cannot see the first child. The third child tries to imitate the position. While the audience enjoys this vastly, the children are learning to use much more accurate descriptive language.

Suggestion(s) for support

Help those who find the activity difficult by selecting simple, one-object pictures, all from the same set. For example, you might use a set of toys (baby board books are a good source of this kind of picture). This cuts out peripheral detail and helps both children in the paired activity. Tell one to say what kind of thing it is: *It is a toy.* Tell him to go on to colour: *It is brown and furry*, and then to give one detail: *It has sticking-up ears.* The second child could ask how the toy moves, where the answer might be: *It runs on all four legs.* This kind of accurate description will give the 'artist' plenty of clues.

Assessment opportunities

Note the children who show that they have listened to the descriptions by, for example, including an unusual detail in their drawings. Note those who use more or less sophisticated language in, for example, their description of colour, shape, similarity.

Display ideas

Make an 'art gallery' display of the original pictures alongside the new versions. Entitle it *'With the ears of an artist'.*

YOU'LL LIKE OUR SCHOOL!

To give young children practice in explaining a situation with which they are familiar.

†† *Several groups (of six to eight), then pairs.*

◷ *15 minutes to organise the task, 5 minutes for each group to carry it out.*

Previous skills/knowledge needed

The children need to have been in school for some time, perhaps a year, to have the necessary experience to pass on to others.

Key background information

This activity concerns a real situation where the children act as guides to groups of new pre-school children and their parents who are coming to look around the school. It is an activity which will help them to become confident in talking to others, including adults, and will enable them to share their experience of school life.

Preparation

This activity demands quite extensive preparation. Make sure that the adults who are to be part of the 'school tour' know when it is going to take place and will be available to talk to the children. Make name badges for both the guides and the new children. (First names only on the badges.)

To organise this activity, divide the class into several groups and allocate a task/topic to each one. Let the children work in pairs on the pre-school open day (usually during the term before the new children come into school), giving each new child and his parents two escorts for each part of the tour.

Resources needed

A flip chart or whiteboard, sticky labels for name badges, one copy per child of photocopiable sheet 142.

What to do

Before the pre-school open day, group around you the children who have been at school for some time. Talk about what they remember and about their feelings when they first started school.

Discuss what they thought school was going to be like and whether it was different – if so in what way? Talk about the colours and the sounds of school, talk about finding one's way around. Think about teachers' names, who belongs in which classroom, what other adults in and around the school do – the caretaker, the secretary, the headteacher, the crossing lady.

Make lists on the flip chart or whiteboard: *People in school, How to find your way, Where things go, Feelings about school.* Scribe and read back some of the ideas that the children have talked about.

Let each of the groups take a separate topic to work on, (one of the above or similar), so that they will be able to talk with confidence about it. Give them the opportunity to do a 'practice run'. Divide each group into pairs and arrange for one pair of children to escort each new child and her or his parents on their allotted part of the tour. Then change over to allow another pair to continue escorting the visitors.

One pair could introduce the visitors to members of staff by name and show them where they work, for example, *'This is Mrs Macaulay. She is the secretary. She helps the head and this is her room.'* Another group can show the newcomers where PE things are kept, where to hang their coats and where assembly takes place. Other places to point out could include the staffroom, toilets, kitchen and caretaker's room.

Another group may talk about their feelings. They should tell the new children about their friends, that parents come to collect you at home time, that Mrs Green makes good dinners (most days!) and so on, trying to make the new children feel that school won't be such an alien experience.

Give out copies of photocopiable sheet 142 for children to record information about their school and its staff, drawing pictures and writing details.

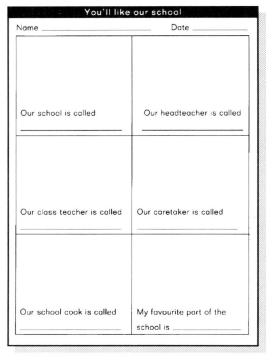

Suggestion(s) for extension

A useful extension to this activity would be to 'twin' your class with one at the same stage in another school. Arrange meetings at both schools, with the hosts again working in pairs, organising a tour of their school. Encourage the children to discuss similarities and differences, perhaps over orange juice and biscuits, or a lunchtime picnic in the grounds. This works best where the schools are in very different locations.

Suggestion(s) for support

Arrange for a shy child to be paired with one who is more confident. Make sure, however, that the less articulate child has just one specific task to carry out –and that both know which task that is!

Assessment opportunities

When overseeing the practice run, ask a few unexpected questions of the children, such as the beginners' parents might ask: *'What do you do if you don't like today's dinner? Who looks after you if you fall in the playground?'* and so on. Make a note of those who can either come up with an answer or have the confidence to say, *'I don't know. Let's ask Mrs Thompson.'* Note those who need help in maintaining a conversation with unfamiliar adults and children.

Display ideas

Make a plan of the school to put up in the hall. The children can make portraits of the teachers, putting them into the correct settings. They can map out how to reach Class 1 from the front door, how to get to the toilets and the assembly hall. Use different-coloured arrows for each route.

Other aspects of the English PoS covered

Reading – 1b, c.
Writing – 1a, b, c; 2e.

Reference to photocopiable sheet

Writing information about (and drawing pictures of) their school and its staff on photocopiable sheet 142 will serve as a record of this activity, and will give the children some experience of filling in forms.

Opinion and persuasion

If you are a parent, you may feel that children need no practice in the art of persuasion! However, they must understand the various contexts in which persuasive language is appropriate, and how best to use it. This chapter has been designed to provide children with various scenarios in which persuasion can be used, where they imagine themselves as advertisers or try to persuade others of a socially desirable outcome – and, of course, use persuasive language to win over parents to their point of view.

It is important that children begin to understand ways in which we try to influence people and the kinds of language we have at our command. They also need to learn how powerful persuasive language can be, and that it can be used equally for good or bad outcomes. This chapter suggests situations in which children can express an opinion and encourages them to think of coherent arguments which will go some way towards convincing others of their point of view. To work through these activities, children also have to learn to listen to the opinions of others, weigh evidence and be able to adjust their point of view in response to other people's ideas and opinion.

SPEAKING AND
LISTENING

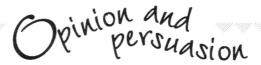

◈ 'I WANT A DRAGON'

***To help children to use the language of persuasion
and to think out plausible arguments.***

†† *Whole class, then groups of four or five.*

🕐 *20 minutes.*

Key background information

This activity is based on what is common practice among
young children: trying to persuade parents/teachers that they
want/need something special! It is important, therefore, to
steer the conversation away from expensive/dangerous
things that parents cannot afford or would not allow for
reasons of safety, to purely imaginative ideas, for example:
*Why can't we have a dinosaur to tea? Please will you buy
me an island?*

Preparation

Make up a graph, ready to show the distribution of pets
among members of the class. Find some dragon poems, for
example: *Dragon Poems,* edited by John Foster (OUP, 1991),
'Breakfast Boast' by Moira Andrew (from *Hammy's House,*
edited by John Foster, OUP, 1992). 'The best pets' (page
93) could be used as a background to this activity.

Resources needed

Dragon pictures in illustrated books, dragon poems, a graph
(see above), sticky paper in different colours cut to fit the
graph, pencils, a flip chart.

What to do

Have the children sitting comfortably and informally in front
of you. Initiate a teacher-led discussion on pets. Listen to
the children's stories about the pets they own, their names,
what funny/naughty things they do, what they like to eat,
how they are looked after.

Find out how many children (or their families) own a cat,
a rabbit, a dog or any other kind of creature. Ask the children
to draw their pet on one of the sticky squares (red for cats,
blue for dogs and so on). Let those who do not have a pet of
their own draw the animal of their choice. Use the graph to
find out which is the most popular pet.

Put the children who don't own a pet into one group. Find
out if they have ever tried to persuade their parents to buy
one. Encourage them to tell the others the reasons why the
parents have said 'No', for example: *too expensive to feed,
vets' fees, too messy, no room in the house, someone's
brother is allergic to dogs, no time to take dogs for a walk,
no pets allowed while there is a baby in the house,* and so
on. Open up the discussion so that the others can add their
ideas.

On the flip chart, note down how many arguments against
owning pets the children have thought about.

Get the children to suggest some really unusual pets which
they would like to have about the house, for example: *a
hippopotamus, a crocodile, an elephant.* Discuss what would
make these animals unsuitable: *too big, out of their
environment, too dangerous.*

Read Moira Andrew's poem 'Breakfast boast' (or another
dragon poem). Show one or two pictures of a dragon. Ask
whether the children think that a dragon would make a good
pet. On the flip chart, note the reasons for and against having
a dragon pet, for example:

▲ **For:** *It would be good for making toast. You wouldn't need
to take it for walks. It could be a guard dragon and frighten
burglars away from the house.*

▲ **Against:** *It might frighten the neighbours. It would set
the smoke alarm off. It might be difficult to find tins of dragon*

food on the supermarket shelves. (The children can have a lot of fun with this idea!)

Having discussed some of the pros and cons, arrange the children in small groups and ask them to think about the arguments they might use to persuade their parents to keep a dragon as a pet. Tell them that you want them to report back in five minutes. You might like to go from group to group listening and offering suggestions.

When the groups are ready, get them to report. On the flip chart note down all the different arguments that they would use to persuade their parents. Review the ways in which the children have used the language of persuasion.

Suggestion(s) for extension

Suggest that more able children think of new 'pets' which they would like to introduce to their homes: *a dinosaur, a unicorn, an elf.* Encourage them to develop persuasive arguments to bring their parents around to their point of view.

Suggest that they think of arguments to be allowed to stay up late, watch a particular video, leave their room to be tidied until the weekend.

Suggestion(s) for support

Suggest that children who need support work with a partner, pairing an able child with one who is less able. The more able child can take the part of the parent, the other can try to argue the case for having a dragon as a pet.

Assessment opportunities

Listen for children who can explore the possibilities in an unfamiliar situation, who can select relevant details to add to their arguments and who can talk, not only persuasively, but coherently. Make a note of the strategies they use.

Opportunities for IT

The children could use graphing or pictogram software as a precursor to this activity. They could collect information about pets, for example how many pets (if any) the children have. This could be used as a basis for the rest of the activity.

Alternatively, if the children can be grouped around a larger screen, the teacher could build up the graph using the

software. This could be a good teaching point for later work by the children.

The children could also use an art package to draw a picture, either of one of their own pets or of an imaginary pet or monster.

Display ideas

Make a wall story with a dragon as the central character. Ask the children to paint a series of pictures in which, for example, the dragon is being taken for a walk, is seen making toast or lighting the family barbecue, is acting as guard dragon with a BEWARE OF THE DRAGON notice prominent on the gate.

Other aspects of the English PoS covered

Reading – 1b, d.
Writing – 1c, 2e.

Performance ideas

From the various arguments they have rehearsed, make up simple drama sequences with the children. Some can take the parts of Mum and Dad, Grandma or Grandad – even the headteacher, who may not want to see a pet dragon in school!

BOX OF WISHES

To help children to express and justify a wish.
†† *Whole class, then three groups.*
🕑 *20 minutes.*

Key background information

This activity leads to imaginative speculation. Children need to be persuaded to leap forward from the banal *Disney World/lots of money* syndrome to thinking of an exciting wish for a world where anything can happen. If the children suggest lots of money, try to lead them on, for example, to the idea of a money tree or a money mountain – imagine walking on a beach made of golden coins instead of pebbles! Give the children the means to imagine quite surreal possibilities.

Resources needed

A tiny colourful, possibly patterned or jewelled box, a scarf, a flip chart or whiteboard.

Opinion and persuasion

What to do

Gather the children around you in the story corner. Keep the box out of sight under the scarf. Ask if anyone can think of a story or a television programme where magic wishes are granted. Listen and talk about their answers.

Suggest that you and they are going to make up a story about three wishes hidden in a magic box – just like *this* one! Reveal the box and let them discuss size, shape and pattern. This focusing of the children's attention on looking closely at the box helps to stimulate the idea that it *might* have various magic properties.

Ask the children to suggest some of the wishes they would make. As they come up with ideas, scribe them on the whiteboard – in no time at all, you will have as many different wishes as you have children in the room!

Remind the children that the box holds only three wishes, so they will have to make a choice. Divide the class into three groups and ask each group to choose one wish. Go from group to group, helping them towards a decision. Encourage everyone to listen to what others in the group have to say. If they choose 'sunshine every day', ask what they would do about the plants if it never rained again – *rain in the night before people get up? Underground wells to water the plants? Plastic plants only?*

When each group has come to a decision, get everybody together and scribe the results on the flip chart. Ask one child from each group to say why they chose that particular wish. The others should listen carefully, be ready to question and argue their own case.

Show the box again and remind the children that it can contain only three wishes. They should now choose three from the original selection on the board. (There should be 12 to 15 ideas, depending on the number of groups.)

Try to persuade the children to come to a consensus: listening, arguing and questioning. You may need to take a vote in the end, but the children will have learned a great deal about the need to take other people's ideas into consideration.

Now, working from the wishes collected on the whiteboard, move the children on to expressing these ideas in the form of a magic wish: *a £10 note tree in the front garden; a pound coin wall round the school; sending beaches to be dry-cleaned; sewing up the hole in the ozone layer with gold thread; holidays on a desert island; a week visiting King Neptune's underwater caves; spending the summer on a spaceship bound for Alpha Centauri and so on.*

Try to ensure that everyone is happy with the final outcome. Show the children the Box of Wishes and pack away each wish, one by one, with an air of mystery. Place the box on the display table along with illustrated traditional or fairy stories. (See 'Display ideas'.)

Suggestion(s) for extension

Put the children into small groups, giving each a small box or beaded bag. Suggest that they imagine that they can choose three dreams, stories, poems, songs or colours to pack into the box or bag. Suggest that they gather these ideas into a list poem, looking something like this:

In the magic bag
I stored three dreams,
dreams of starlight,
dreams of rainbows,
dreams of mountains.
I closed the bag,
tied the top tight,
so my dreams
could not escape.

Children who are independent writers can write their poem inside a 'magic bag or box' shape (see illustration). An adult can scribe for the others and the children can copy the poem. Using the same format, the children could substitute 'stories' or 'memories' for 'dreams'.

Suggestion(s) for support

Make it easier for those children who need support by pairing them with a more able child. Suggest that the confident child lead his or her partner towards three simple ideas, showing why each idea might make a good choice.

Assessment opportunities

Look for the language of speculation: *I think... Wouldn't it be a good idea if...? Perhaps... How would you like it if...?* Listen for the children who use these phrases easily and confidently, knowing how to use them effectively when putting over a point of view.

Display ideas

Cover a display table with attractive drapes and place the patterned box in a prominent position. Surround it with a number of illustrated picture books, open at a 'magic' page, preferably one where wishes are being answered.

On a frieze above the table, get the children to paint or colour a large version of the Box of Wishes, with the lid slightly lifted. Show each wish on a streamer floating into the box. Make it look as magical as possible with additions of gold and silver streaks around the box. The children might also like to add magic wands, with gold stars on top. (See illustration above.)

Other aspects of the English PoS covered

Reading – 1c, d.
Writing – 1c; 2b, e.

PAINT YOUR DRAGON

To help children to articulate their thoughts and reasons and to use the language of persuasion to bring others round to their point of view.

†† *Whole class, then four more or less equal-sized groups.*

⏱ *20 minutes.*

Key background information

This activity relies on chance to make allocations, then requires the children to find good reasons why theirs is the best. (It in some ways replicates what happens when children are allocated randomly to a particular group and immediately find good reasons why theirs is the best!) Encourage the children to think about unusual reasons why a blue dragon might be better than a red/yellow/green one, for example: *He is the colour of the sky, so if he stands still nobody will see him.*

Preparation

Make up four narrow cards (markers) in red, blue, green and yellow, coloured on one side only. Find some books with illustrations of dragons. *Dragon Poems* edited by John Foster (OUP, 1991) is very colourful and much loved by children. *The Paper Bag Princess* by Robert N. Munsch (Hippo Books, 1982) is an amusingly illustrated and thought-provoking dragon story.

Resources needed

Coloured pencils (red, blue, green, yellow), one copy per child of photocopiable page 143, dragon pictures, coloured markers (see above).

What to do

Gather the children together in the story corner. Look at the illustrations of dragons and discuss their features: tail, wings, spikes. Ask for the children's ideas about whether or not dragons have ever existed and encourage them to talk about where they think dragons might have lived: *in caves, on the top of a mountain* and so on. Ask if they know any dragon stories or songs. Read from *Dragon Poems*.

Arrange the children into four equal groups. Check that they all know to which group they belong, then produce the coloured markers. Place these colour side down and ask a child from each group to choose one. When they have done so, tell them that they can find their own special dragon-colour by looking at the marker. The children should disperse into their groups, where each child should colour the photocopied dragon picture, using red, blue, green or yellow depending on the group marker.

Go round to each group and ask them to think of three reasons why their dragon-colour is best, for example: *Red is the best colour because it means DANGER and our dragon is dangerous! Yellow is the best colour because it is a happy colour and our dragon is always happy. Green is the best colour because it makes it easy for dragons to hide in the long grass* – and so on. The reasons can be quite zany or bizarre, using the logic of fantasy. Give the children ten minutes to colour in their pictures and think of three good reasons why their dragon-colour is the best, then get them to sit back in the story corner.

Each group should be able to explain to the others why they think that their colour is the best. If children hesitate, be ready to help them out. Make this a fun activity, with children always remaining aware that dragons are figments of the imagination and that their reasons, therefore, do not need to be too realistic.

If one group manages to persuade a child from another group that its dragon-colour is best, that child can move to join it. Clap each group in turn as the children put forward their ideas.

After each group has put forward their 'red/green is the best colour' ideas, help the children to consider why they came to these conclusions. They may say something like 'Well, I'm in the red group, so it must be best!' Discuss with them how they would have felt if, for example, they had been

in the yellow group. Remind the children that they chose their colours at random – they couldn't see which colour they were selecting. Talk a little about other things that we can't choose, such as whether we are boys or girls, or the colour of our skin. Try not to be too 'heavy' about this discussion, but help the children to begin to think about prejudice.

Suggestion(s) for extension

Suggest that the children might think of other 'magic' colours for dragons – why, for example, a golden/silver/rainbow dragon might be best of all! Again, they should be able to articulate three good reasons why. Let the children paint a dragon of their choice.

Another possible idea is to ask more able children in the extension group to think of a new colour for a real animal – why might a green elephant be better than an ordinary grey one? How about a blue-spotted fish? Or a bright red snail?

Suggestion(s) for support

If there are some children who cannot make the imaginative jump required by this activity, ask an adult helper to work with a small group of perhaps three or four, helping them to think of fairly mundane reasons why a red dragon is best, for example: *You can see it from a long way off. Red is the brightest colour. Red is the same colour as fire.*

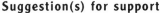

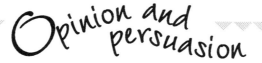

Assessment opportunities
Note those children who are able to put forward a group point of view, *We think that red is best because ...* Ask one of the less articulate ones if he can think of another reason, and listen to check whether he can construct a reasoning sentence using *because* correctly.

Display ideas
After they have coloured the photocopied pictures, encourage the children to paint or colour dragons free-hand. Cut them out and mount on a fantastic background of icy mountains. Title the frieze *HERE BE DRAGONS – BEWARE!*

Other aspects of the English PoS covered
Reading – 1d.

Reference to photocopiable sheet
Photocopiable sheet 143 is used as a resource in the game described above. It could also be used to stimulate discussion about types of dragon: Chinese dragons, Welsh dragons and so on.

Performance ideas
The children can make dragon masks in their group colour. They can make up a group chant, for example: *We are the red dragons. We are the colour of fire! We are the colour of the sky at night. We are DANGEROUS! We are the red dragons on the march. BEWARE!* The groups can perform to a percussion accompaniment – with a cymbal crash at the end.

I FEEL BLUE

To help children to express opinions about their feelings and to encourage them to listen to and consider the opinions of others.
†† *Whole class.*
🕐 *25 minutes.*

Previous skills/knowledge needed
The children may need to be happy with the idea of talking about their emotions – sadness, loneliness, fear, for example.

Key background information
This activity deals very directly with the children's feelings, so the discussion needs to be dealt with in a sensitive way. Watch out for anyone who retreats into silence, especially if this is not their usual behaviour.

Preparation
Cut coloured paper or card into playing card-sized rectangles. Try to provide an interesting range of colours, not just blue, green, yellow but pink, turquoise and purple. Add silver and gold – even cards made from shaded paper. Look out a selection of poems which express how children might feel in different situations, for example: 'Baby' by Paul Rogers (new baby arriving in the family) in *Another Very First Poetry Book* ed. John Foster (OUP, 1992); 'The Shadow Man' by John Foster (night-time fear) in *My Red Poetry Book* ed. Moira Andrew (Nelson, 1988); 'Stepmother' by Jean Kenward (new parent) in *All In the Family* ed. John Foster (OUP, 1993).

Resources needed
'Feelings' poems marked ready to read, coloured cards, a flip chart, one copy per child of photocopiable sheet 144, coloured pencils.

What to do
Gather the children in the story corner. Put four coloured cards (red, blue, green, yellow) face down on the floor. Tell the children that you are going to play a game. Ask one child to pick a card, but not let anyone else see its colour. Say

that she must not tell what colour she has chosen, but that the others must guess from a clue such as *My card is the colour of the sun.* Now suggest that the children think of a fruit, a flower, a pudding that is always yellow: *a banana, a buttercup* and *custard.* Encourage the children to think of as many yellow things as they can.

Go on to work in a similar way with the other three cards.

Now hold up one of the cards. Ask the children this time to think of how the colour makes them feel: happy, lonely, frightened, sad. Let them discuss it and air their opinions, always ensuring that they keep to the rules of taking turns and listening to what the other children have to say.

Put a blue blob on the flip chart. From a show of hands, count how many think blue is a sad, happy or lonely colour. Write the number beside the appropriate feeling word. Has what children have said changed anyone's mind? Why?

Now read two or three of the poems you have selected. Ask at the end how they made the children feel? Have they thought of new feeling words? For example: jealous, angry, excited. Discuss what happens to make them feel this way. Listen carefully to their stories and try to defuse any problems or difficulties.

Produce the other coloured cards. Ask the children to think of silver or golden feelings, of how black, purple or a shaded card makes them feel.

Put all the cards on the floor, face-up this time. Let each child choose one and give them time to talk about what the colour means to them. Ask them to begin: *I feel blue when ... I feel silver when ...* and so on, expressing both their feelings and their opinions in terms of colour.

Give out the photocopies of page 144. Suggest that the children look at the pictures and think about how each child is feeling. Using coloured pencils, they can shade in the background in what they consider to be an appropriate 'feeling' colour. Encourage them to write 'He feels blue because he is sad,' and so on, copying text from the whiteboard.

Suggestion(s) for extension

More able children could make up a chant, beginning:

Yellow (or green/red) is for bananas and custard.
Yellow is for sunflowers and lemons.
Yellow is for the sun and moon.
Yellow is for when I feel very CROSS
    with my baby brother!

The children can work either individually or as a group. An adult can scribe the finished chant as a wall-poem.

Suggestion(s) for support

Work individually with children who need support, using only the basic four cards: blue, yellow, red and green. Encourage them to form simple sentences like: *Red is when I'm angry. Yellow is when I'm happy.* Scribe the sentences and get the children to copy them out on the relevant coloured cards.

Assessment opportunities

Assessment is difficult in this activity. Some children can speak articulately about their feelings, but won't. Others would like to talk, but are inhibited by lack of language with which to express feelings. Encourage those children to talk

about something that happened recently to make them feel happy – for example, *going to buy sweets with Grandma, feeding the ducks in the park, beating my big sister at Ludo.* Follow up by helping the children to explore *how* being happy feels, and so on. Develop a question-and-answer process, being sensitive to how far it is appropriate to proceed with each individual child.

Opportunities for IT

The children could use a word processor to write one of their colour lines, such as 'I feel yellow when I am happy.' As the text is quite short, they will be able to complete a simple piece of word processing fairly quickly. If the class has access to a colour printer, they could be shown how to change the colour of their sentence. They should print out the text when it is finished, and it can be used as part of a class display.

Display ideas

Make a huge colour wheel. Get children to write out single words on white using an appropriately coloured felt-tipped pen: *ANGRY! CROSS! SAD!* and so on. Cut out the words and glue them onto the correct segments of the wheel. (See illustration above.)

SPEAKING AND LISTENING

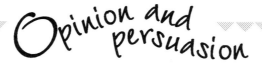
Other aspects of the English PoS covered
Reading – 1c, d.
Writing – 1b; 2b, e.

Reference to photocopiable sheet
The pictures on photocopiable sheet 144 depict the emotional states of sadness, anticipation, amusement and fear.

LITTERBUGS

To help children to use the language of persuasion with clarity and precision towards a socially desirable outcome.

†† *Whole class, followed by three groups.*

🕐 *30 minutes.*

Previous skills/knowledge needed
It helps if the children realise that it is unacceptable to throw litter around, but specific training is unnecessary.

Preparation
It would be useful if you could get your hands on posters or literature distributed by environmental groups who are concerned to educate young children about keeping the environment clean and tidy. Arrange for two or three children to pick up 'clean' litter from the playground after break (especially effective on a windy day). The children should wear plastic gloves and put the litter in clean bin bags. The caretaker might be happy to supervise this part of the activity.

Resources needed
Plastic gloves, black bin bags, examples of 'clean' litter (crisp bags, sweet wrappers, bus tickets), a plastic sheet, backing paper and glue for the children's posters, a flip chart, photographs or book illustrations of town, country and seaside scenes, a few advertisements, anti-litter posters. One copy per child of the photocopiable summative assessment sheet on page 145 (if required).

What to do
With the children sitting in front of you, show first a picture or a photograph of an idyllic country scene. Ask the children to think about what they see in the picture, what makes it beautiful, for example: trees, sunshine, sparkling river, sheep on the hillside, green fields, hedgerows.

Display and discuss an urban picture in the same way. It may show shops, houses with gardens, mums pushing prams, cars, people queuing at the bus stop and so on. Introduce a seaside picture and again encourage the children to comment on what they can see in it.

Wearing plastic gloves, empty the bag of litter on to the plastic sheet. Suggest that the children think what difference this litter would make to the three scenes they have been

looking at and talking about. Listen to their comments and try to draw their attention to the effect of, for example, plastic drinks bottles on the waves (*What happens to plastic bottles? Do they sink or float?*), glass bottles in the sand (*Why are they dangerous?*). Ask them to make suggestions about what we *should* do with litter: *put it in the bins, take it home, put glass and plastic bottles in the green bags.* Encourage a positive approach.

Ask the children if they know what an advert is. Where do we see advertisements? – *on television, in newspapers, on hoardings.* Explore with them ideas about what an advertisement tries to do – *it makes you want to buy things, it tells you how good some things (toys, ice-cream, breakfast cereals, sweets) are.* Suggest that sometimes advertisements try to persuade people *not* to do things. Show and discuss the anti-litter posters.

Ask the children to think of what they would say to get people *not* to throw litter around. Put some of their ideas on the flip chart and get them to read back, for example: *Don't drop litter. Litter makes a mess. Litter makes places ugly. Litter can be dangerous. Keep the playground/street/ countryside/beach clean!*

Arrange the children in three groups. Give each one picture and a few scraps of litter. Get the groups to talk about how they would go about making an anti-litter poster. What words

would they use? What pictures would they paint? How would they use the pieces of litter?

Ask the children to report back to the class. Then suggest that each group makes its own anti-litter poster.

Suggestion(s) for extension

Suggest that a more able group talks about what they would say to other children in the school to persuade them not to throw litter around. Once they have done this, they could go to another class with their posters and their slogans to campaign against litter in the playground.

Suggestion(s) for support

Work in small groups with the children who need support. First, make sure that they know what litter is. Reinforce the need to put litter in public bins or to take it home. Ask them

- sweet wrappers
- cut-out eyes with buttons
- Smartie tube
- empty can
- newspaper
- egg carton

to say why this is the right thing to do. Get them to work with a partner, explaining the problem and persuading them not to throw crisp packets and so on around. They might like to be recruited as playground litter-guards!

Assessment opportunities

This activity can be used for summative assessment, and photocopiable sheet 145 is provided for this purpose. Note the children's ability to think ahead: *if* litter is left around, *then* there will be a predictable outcome. Note their ability to use language in a persuasive, not a hectoring, way. Listen for evidence (in the relevance and appropriateness of their responses) that they have listened carefully.

Opportunities for IT

Some groups could use an art package to create and draw their litter posters. They could be shown how to add text (anti-litter slogans) to the picture. Alternatively, the children

could use a word processor or a simple desk-top publishing package to write the slogan in large print, which could then be printed out; the rest of the poster could be drawn in by hand. It might also be possible to scan in children's own line drawings, so that the whole poster can be completed using the computer.

Display ideas

Put the children's anti-litter posters up in the classroom or in the assembly hall. Make *Litterbugs!*– that is, cartoon people using cast-off cartons, packets, tickets and various wrappings to make the figures. The lids from bottles make good staring eyes, milk bottle tops make sticking-out ears and a 'Smartie' tube makes a mouth. (See illustration.)

Other aspects of the English PoS covered

Reading – 1c.

Performance ideas

The children can improvise role-play, for example, careless adult/sensible child, to reinforce the need to look after the environment and think carefully about what we do with our litter.

Reference to photocopiable sheet

Photocopiable sheet 145 can be used for summative assessment of the children's ability to persuade and express opinions, based on this activity.

THE BEST PETS

To help children to express a choice and argue its validity.

†† *Whole class, then groups of four or five.*

🕐 *20–25 minutes.*

Key background information

This activity depends on children making an informed choice concerning the ideal pet. The small groups should be made up of children who all choose a particular pet; dog group, cat group, budgie group and so on. Of course, the groups may well be unequal, so you may have two cat groups and only a couple of children in the goldfish group. Try to even them out if you can. Encourage the children to present a fair point of view, for example, cats can look after themselves, but dogs need to be walked twice a day – not: *Well, I think cats are best because my cat is a nice cat.*

Preparation

Make an enlarged copy of photocopiable sheet 146, so that all the children can see it easily. Ask the children to bring in photographs of their pets. (Label the photographs on the back so that they do not get lost.)

Resources needed

An enlarged copy of photocopiable page 146, one copy per child of photocopiable page 146 and page 147 (if required), children's photographs, photo corners, a large sheet of card, a flip chart. Perhaps a photograph of your own pet, if you have one.

What to do

Gather the children's photographs and keep them in a safe place. Arrange to have the children sit comfortably in the story corner and ask them if they have stories to tell about their pets, for example, the funniest thing it ever did. Ask each contributor to tell what kind of pet they have, its name, something about what it looks like (colour, size). Listen to and comment on the stories, encouraging the other children to ask relevant questions.

Leave time to talk with those children who do not have a pet, asking them to choose the ideal pet – and explain why. Again, encourage listening, questions and comment.

Ask the children to put up their hands if they own a cat, a dog, a bird, a goldfish, anything different. (Those who have more than one must choose the pet they like best.) Put the results (as numbers) on the flip chart. Make a separate list for the children who wish they had a pet.

Now group the children according to the pet they think is best, so that you may have a dog group, two cat groups, a goldfish group and so on. Identify each group with a picture (perhaps taken from the enlarged copy of page 146) of the appropriate pet. Tell them to think of three things that make their kind of pet the best. Give them three or four minutes.

Bring the children back into a whole-class discussion. Try to get each group to be fairly precise about why they think a particular kind of pet is the most desirable. Encourage each group to try and convince those without pets of the reasons why their kind of pet is best. Encourage positive all-encompassing answers, for example: *Dogs are best because they bark at burglars. Goldfish are best because they don't scratch the furniture.*

Scribe a list of 'good things' about each pet on the flip chart. Use the children's photographs to make up books or classroom displays about each kind of pet, noting the various types of cats and dogs. Let the children copy or write independently about the good points of their own kind of pet. (See 'Display ideas').

Give each child a photocopied picture (perhaps taken from page 146) of the pet of her or his choice. They could colour these and cut them out to make a collective bar chart of the best pets.

Suggestion(s) for extension

Get more capable children to talk about what kind of pet would be best to have around the house from a list of mythical creatures (for example, dragons, unicorns, trolls) or from a list of dinosaurs; or they could invent their own creature. They can draw and describe their imaginary pet on photocopiable sheet 147.

Suggestion(s) for support

Work with small groups of less able children, encouraging them to suggest one good thing about a dog or a cat. Put them into two groups and encourage them to put over their point of view in a clear way.

Assessment opportunities

Listen to the variety of language used in describing the pets, in storytelling, in presenting a point of view.

Opportunities for IT

The children could use graphing or pictogram software to create a graph of the class's pets. They could also use a word processor to give the three reasons why they think their pet is the best. They could print this out, leaving space for a picture or photograph brought from home. It might also be possible to scan pictures brought from home, so that the children can complete the whole task using the computer – in which case, they need to think about where on the page they will place the picture and the text.

A more ambitious project for older children would be to make a multimedia presentation about the 'best' class pets, using simple authoring software. The children could work in 'best pet' groups. The teacher could set up the framework, with perhaps a title page giving a list of the pets to be covered – so that clicking on *dogs*, for example, would take the children to their pages about dogs. On these pages, the children in the group could add pictures of their own dogs, drawn using an art package or scanned from their own photographs or line drawings. By clicking on a question mark, the children would be taken to a page where they can

give their reasons in writing why theirs in the best pet to keep. They could also add their voices, recorded using a microphone attached to the computer, giving the reasons; they could even add a recorded sound of a dog barking. This kind of work needs to be carefully planned and spread over an extended period, so that the children have enough time to complete the different parts of the presentation. The support of another adult will usually be needed to help and guide children in the work.

Display ideas

Make large floor books about dogs, cats, birds and so on, as suggested above.

Ask the children to paint (or draw using oil-based crayons) a large picture of each desirable pet, real or imagined. These should be cut out and pasted, collage-fashion, on a Pet Show frieze.

Other aspects of the English PoS covered

Reading – 1b; 2a.
Writing – 1b, c; 2e.

Reference to photocopiable sheets

Sheet 146 shows six different kinds of pet for the children to identify and discuss. Sheet 147 (see Extension) invites children to draw and describe an imaginary pet.

Performance ideas

The children can make simple animal masks and wear them to present a *We are the best pets!* parade for other classes in the school. They should make use of the ideas which they presented earlier in the activity.

FANTASTIC! WONDERFUL!

To help children understand something about what effect advertisements have and to help them use the language of persuasion for themselves.

†† *Whole class, then pairs, followed by four equal groups.*

🕐 *30 minutes.*

Previous skills/knowledge needed

Most young children are already aware of advertising, mainly through the medium of television.

Key background information

This activity is in two distinct parts. The first part encourages the children to think about the power of advertising and the persuasive effect it may have on them. The second part gives children the opportunity to try out their ideas for persuasion on others.

Preparation

Ask children to look at home for advertisements for sweets, food or toys in old magazines or newspapers, and to bring examples into school along with some empty cereal packets. (Otherwise, bring these in yourself.) Cover four packets (one for each group) with plain paper. In felt-tipped pen mark each with a made-up name for a new cereal: *Sparkles, Wheetipops* and so on.

Resources needed

Advertisements and empty cereal packets (marked as suggested above), felt-tipped pens.

SPEAKING AND LISTENING

What to do

Gather the children together on the carpet, each with a cut-out advert and an empty cereal packet. Ask them to put these on the floor in front of them and think first about the adverts they see on television.

Discuss with them first those adverts that make them laugh. What was amusing in them? *Cartoon characters doing funny things, children getting the better of their parents, children saying or doing things that they are not allowed to do ...* and so on. Go on to probe whether the children appreciate that advertisements are trying to make them want particular things to wear, eat or play with. Ask the children which toy they would like to have most in the world (if money was not important). Discuss why they want it. How many others would like to have the same thing? Find out where they first got to know about it – does some other child have one or did they see it advertised on television? (Most will probably say they have seen it on TV, especially just before Christmas!)

Get the children to think about their own favourite advertisements. Can they say what they like about them? Is it the characters, the pictures, the jingle or what the advert is selling? Find out which is the class's favourite advert.

Ask the children to hold up their empty cereal packets. Get them to move into separate 'product' groups. When they have settled, ask the children to think about how they knew so quickly which group to join. Were any children unable to decide which group they belonged to?

Demonstrate that many of the children, without reading or being able to read, know immediately the *'Cornflakes'* group from the *'Rice Krispies'* group and so on. Establish that they recognise the format and pictures on the box. Get them to talk about the differences between packets.

Now ask the children to think about the cut-out adverts which they have brought. How many advertise sweets? food? toys? The children should look at their adverts with a partner, working out what they think each advert is trying to do. Does it make them want to spend their pocket money on it? eat the sweets? play with the toy? wear the shoes? After five minutes, they should report back to the main group.

Divide the children into four groups, giving each a cereal box with its made-up name. Tell them that they have invented a new breakfast cereal. Ask them to decide what is special about it: *sweet, crunchy, chocolatey or something else?* Ask the children to finish decorating the box with felt-tipped pens. Then get each group to tell the others how wonderful their new cereal is. They should try to persuade everyone to think that theirs is the best. Encourage the use of suitable adjectives – *super, cool, wonderful, marvellous, fantastic!* and whatever the current expression is.

Suggestion(s) for extension

Ask more able children to choose their favourite book from the library shelf. Get them to think about how they could 'sell' it to the others. They should think of five really good things to say about it which would persuade other children to read it.

Suggestion(s) for support

Children who find the activity difficult should work in twos. Let each pair choose one of the packets of cereal (which they would enjoy eating) and think of five things that they like about the product. Suggest that they tell the others why they think it is so good.

Assessment opportunities

Note those children who are able to present their ideas and preferences to others with confidence. Listen to the children's use of persuasive language.

Display ideas

Use large sheets of sugar paper to make advertisements for the made-up cereals. First, ask the children for their choice of adjectives and write them on the flip chart. Then let the children copy some of the words onto their own adverts. (Some may like to think of new words and phrases.) Use

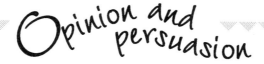

bold felt-tipped pens for this part of the activity, encouraging large clear printing. Get the children to draw and colour in bowls of cereal.

Other aspects of the English PoS covered
Reading – 1b, c.
Writing – 1c, 2b.

Performance ideas
Encourage the children to make up a 'television' advert for their favourite sweets/toys/breakfast cereal. Introduce a character to extol its virtues and get the children to make up a catchy jingle to go with the advert.

WHAT HAVE YOU DONE?

To help children to put forward a point of view in group discussion.

†† *Whole class.*

🕐 *20 minutes.*

Previous skills/knowledge needed
An ability to make deductions from information contained in pictures. The activity 'What's happening?' (page 75) could be used as preparation.

Key background information
This activity relies on children being able to form an opinion based solely on pictures. Encourage them to build up a believable background to go with the illustrations. Once they have done this, they must be able to persuade others of the validity of their point of view. This activity tends to become quite lively, so insist on the rules of listening to others and raising hands.

Preparation
Invent your own scenario for the characters in the illustrations. Make enlarged copies of photocopiable sheet 148, so that the pictures can be seen easily by everybody in the class.

Resources needed
A flip chart or whiteboard, one copy per child of photocopiable sheet 148.

What to do
Ask the children to think about a situation in which Mum, Dad or a teacher might say something like, *And what have you been doing?* Make your voice sound quite cross and accusatory, so that there is no doubt that the adult is not best pleased! Listen to the stories the children tell about, for example, *once when I came home with my trousers torn ..., once when I lost my new hair-band ..., once when I scratched the paint on my bike ...* and so on.

Ask the children to think about why Mum/Dad/the teacher was cross. What clues did they have in the adult's response? Discuss their answers.

Now show the children the first of the four pictures on the photocopiable sheet (the dirty, bedraggled child and dog). Ask them to think about the clues they can see. The child is wet, muddy and dirty with torn jeans. Ask them to think about where he or she has been, about what he or she has been doing. Do they think Mum was right to ask *'What have you been doing?'* in that tone of voice?

SPEAKING AND LISTENING

From their replies, try to build a consensus of opinion. (The child has obviously been in the water: lake? puddle? stream?) How did the jeans come to be torn? And what about the dog?

Get the children to build up a scenario, for example: child sees dog in stream, tries to rescue him, can't reach, falls in, tears jeans on a branch and so on. Encourage individuals to argue their case – for example, the child is wet, so any idea that does not take this fact into consideration should be discarded.

Scribe the finished 'story' on the flip chart or whiteboard.

Follow a similar procedure with the other pictures, always encouraging informed debate.

Suggestion(s) for extension

Put the children into groups of four or five and give them a photograph, a story-book picture or one illustration cut from a comic sequence. It is important that the pictures/ photographs have no accompanying text, so that the children have to work out what is happening simply from visual clues. Ask the children to work on the illustration as a group, making up a story to go with the action. Scribe the finished story on the flip chart and ask them to tell/ explain it to the other children in the class.

Suggestion(s) for support

Work with a small group, taking them through the picture step-by-step, emphasising each clue as it arises, for example: the wet child, torn clothes, scruffy dog.

Assessment opportunities

Listen closely to the arguments individual children put forward. Note those who use factual evidence and are able to convince others of the validity of their interpretation, simply using picture clues. Note, too, those who can move on to more imaginative ideas based on the facts. These children may well become excellent storytellers and good writers.

Display ideas

Divide the completed stories into sections and get the children to illustrate each part in paint, wax crayon or coloured pencil. Scribe the text below the pictures, with Mum in the final picture saying in a speech bubble, comic-style, *What have you been doing?* Make the cartoons into wall stories.

Other aspects of the English PoS covered

Reading – 2c.

Writing – 1c.

Reference to photocopiable sheet

Photocopiable sheet 148 presents a sequence of pictures which can be used to tell a story. The children have to develop the story through role play, inferring motives and attitudes which could underlie the events.

Performance ideas

The children can develop each storyline into a short play to be performed to other classes in the school or to parents.

Reasoning and speculating

The ability to predict an outcome and make deductions through discussion of possibilities is an important linguistic skill. It enables us to come to a conclusion, to make choices and to evaluate the reasons for these choices. Children should begin to understand that predictive language is patterned, and that one can make deductions from the way in which people talk and behave. They should learn that things tend to happen in a particular sequence and that they can use their previous experience of, for example, story endings to predict how a particular story might conclude.

This chapter is designed to provide the children with a range of different contexts which they are encouraged to explore, using the twin skills of speculative language and listening to the ideas expressed by others. They are asked to use these contexts as background for discussion, so that they can make an educated guess at the possible outcome of a particular situation. They are expected to give clear reasons for their choices.

The children are encouraged to use elimination and predictive techniques to develop their ideas, and to explore new and unusual situations. In some of the activities (such as 'Feathers in the sky'), they are invited to make an imaginative leap and to share and discuss way-out inventions and ideas with other members of the class.

THE WHOLE PICTURE

To encourage children to make deductions and to help them to explain their reasons in clear language.

†† *Whole class, followed by groups of five or six.*

🕐 *25 minutes.*

Previous skills/knowledge needed
The children require some knowledge about different animals, perhaps from picture books and television programmes.

Key background information
This activity relies on the children's ability to piece together different bits of information which may appear unrelated. It is important to move the session along, making sure that everyone has a chance to make a guess. Be ready with new clues so that the children can begin to eliminate possibilities and reach the correct conclusion. One note of warning: this activity can be rather noisy!

Preparation
Look for illustrated books of animals. Blank off part of each picture, using cut paper as a temporary mask – paperclip or Blu-tack the masks in place. Delete, for example, head and tail or feet and horns, so that the children can use the remaining parts of the picture as clues to guess the animal. (In general, the head should be covered – otherwise, identifications will be too easy.) Prepare some oral clues, along the lines suggested below.

Resources needed
Illustrated animal books with pictures partially blanked off with paper masking (as described above), one copy per child of photocopiable sheet 149, scissors, coloured pencils, a jigsaw puzzle.

What to do
Gather the children together in the story corner. When they are settled, ask if they know what a detective does. Most will be aware that a detective helps to catch criminals. Emphasise the idea that in order to do this, a detective has to work from clues or pieces of 'evidence'.

Show the children some pieces from a jigsaw puzzle. Ask if they can work out what the whole jigsaw might show; encourage them to think about how, once two or three pieces are matched, they can begin to use these 'clues' to work out the puzzle. Tell them that they are going to use some clues like this to guess the animals you are thinking about.

Say, for example, *'The animal I'm thinking about has four legs.'* Ask the children if they can guess what it is – of course they may do so, but at a wild guess, so give another clue. *'This animal lives in the jungle.'* *'Is it a jaguar?'* the children might ask. Encourage questions and answer them to provide further clues. *'Can the animal run fast?'* *'What does it like to eat?'* *'What colour is its coat?'* *'Does it have stripes?'* *'Yes.'* Now all the hands will be up.

Reflect with the children on the way in which they followed your clues (like detectives). Show how they eliminated other creatures by moving nearer and nearer to the correct answer.

Now move on to give clues about a different creature. *'The creature I'm thinking about has no legs.'* Again give clues which help to eliminate fish, jellyfish, eels, worms and so on, until the children come to the answer, *'It's a snake!'* Of course, you can work through different kinds of snake until you get to *rattlesnake, adder* or *boa-constrictor*, but that may become too sophisticated.

After you have worked through a number of oral clues, move on to picture clues. Show the children one of the masked illustrations, encouraging them to make deductions from the information they can see. Get them to explain clearly why they have concluded that it is a picture of an elephant, for example, from the shape and colour of one foot and a tail.

Give each group a masked picture and suggest that they guess the identity of the creature by using the visual clues. After a few minutes, the children should report back to the main group and be able to say how they came to their conclusions.

To complete the session, give each child a copy of photocopiable page 149 and ask them to work out what the whole picture, in each of the first three boxes, might show. They should draw in the missing parts and be able to say why they made those decisions. In the last box, each child should draw part of a new picture and pass it on to another child for completion. The children should attempt to complete each other's pictures without discussion – if possible.

Suggestion(s) for extension

Work in pairs. Give each child a discarded picture (perhaps from comics or old reading books). Get them to cut it into two irregular parts and hide the smaller part. Then they should paste the cut picture on to blank paper and ask their partner to draw in the missing part. They must be able to say what clues they used.

Suggestion(s) for support

Let children who find this activity difficult work one-to-one with an adult helper, if possible. Give them a simple cut picture, asking them to draw in the missing section. Encourage them to talk through what they are doing with the adult, who can give helpful clues if the child gets stuck.

Assessment opportunities

Note the level of reasoning used. Have the children used all the clues given? Can they use the language of deduction and elimination to come to a satisfactory conclusion?

Opportunities for IT

Older or more able children could use a branching database to complement this activity. This type of database differs from conventional ones in that the children must initially 'teach' the software about the different animals by phrasing questions that can only be answered with *Yes* or *No*. Answering *Yes* to a question leads in one direction, *No* in another. This links the activity very closely to the speaking and listening aspect of this work. The resulting key can be used by other children to identify any objects in the set of animals.

For example, a branching database could start:

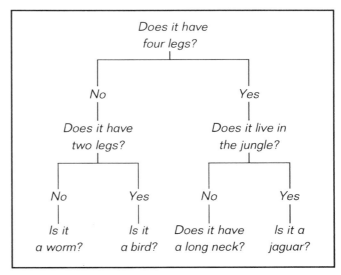

The activity is best organised in small groups, starting off with a limited range of animals. An important part of the

activity is to decide on the first question, which will provide a good basis for splitting the set of animals. Younger children will need initial help, especially in reading the questions and entering the answers.

Display ideas
Suggest that the children create a *Crazy Zoo*. First, they can paint a number of different animals. When the paintings are dry, they can be cut up, so that, for example, a camel gets an elephant's head, a giraffe's long neck is attached to a lion's body and so on. Make a zoo background and put the crazy creatures on display.

Reference to photocopiable sheet
Suggest that the children work in pairs, discussing how they have used their 'detection' ability to work out what each of

the three pictures shows and what is missing. In the last box, each child should draw part of a picture and pass it on to her partner, who should try to complete the scene.

HOLIDAY PHOTOGRAPHS

To encourage children to make clear choices and to help them to give reasons. To encourage children to listen and remember.

✝✝ *Whole class, then four fairly equal groups.*
🕐 *30 minutes.*

Previous skills/knowledge needed
The children need to have some experience of getting ready to go on holiday, and knowledge of clothes suitable for different kinds of weather.

Key background information
Part of this activity (where children repeat and develop a story) is related to the game of 'Chinese whispers' and relies on the children's ability to listen and remember.

Preparation
Find some commercial catalogues with advertisements for children's clothes and toys. Ask the children each to bring in one holiday photograph, if possible. The activity 'You won't believe this!' (page 67) could be used to introduce the 'Chinese whispers' idea.

Resources needed
Holiday brochures, catalogues and holiday photographs (as suggested above), an empty suitcase, one copy per child of photocopiable sheet 150.

What to do

Ask the children to take their holiday photographs into the story corner. When everyone is seated quietly and comfortably, ask two fairly confident children to come to the front. Ask them each to show their photograph to the others. Encourage them to say where the photograph was taken (if they remember!) and what they were doing at the time. What else did they do that day? Try to give this opportunity to as many of the class as possible. By using open questions, encourage descriptive language, especially about photographs in which children are in an unusual situation, for example: in fancy dress, with ice-cream covered faces, squinting at the sun.

Following on from the photograph session, discuss with the children different kinds of holiday destination, for example: holidays at the seaside, in a tent or caravan, foreign holidays (and the excitement of travelling by plane). Some children may take holidays at home, visiting museums and theme parks, others may have been ski-ing or sailing. (Be sensitive to children whose experience of holidays may have been adversely affected by family or economic circumstances.)

Use the brochures to extend the children's ideas about weather, holiday activities and so on. Now bring out the empty suitcase, open it and suggest that if they were going on holiday tomorrow and could each choose one thing to pack, what would it be? Encourage them to vary their answers, then ask them to give a reason for their choice: *I'm going to take a bathing costume, so that I can swim in the sea. I'll take my teddy, because he would be lonely if I left him at home. I'll take my bucket and spade to build the biggest sandcastle in the world!* and so on.

Divide the children into four groups and give each a catalogue. Suggest that each group is going on a different kind of holiday; for example: by plane to a sunny place, to the snow, camping, to the seaside. Each child must choose to take one thing, all different, suitable for that particular holiday. (No swimsuits on the winter holiday!) Let them use the catalogue to give them ideas. Make this a very quick exercise, giving them just a few minutes to make up their minds.

Bring the groups back together. Choose one to start and suggest a formula sentence for the first child: *I went on holiday to a sunny place and I packed my swimsuit.* The next child must try to remember what went before so that he can say: *I went on holiday to a sunny place and I packed my swimsuit and my sunglasses.* Then *I went on holiday to a sunny place and I packed my swimsuit and my sunglasses and my camera* and so on. It gets more difficult as the activity progresses, but allow the children to help one another out if they get stuck. Do the same with the other groups, for example: *I went on holiday in a tent and I packed my sleeping bag...* The children enjoy the challenge of trying to remember what went before.

Give out the copies of photocopiable sheet 150. Suggest that the children draw in 'colour photographs' of themselves on holiday in the place (from the brochures) that they like best of all. Encourage them to think of something funny or interesting or exciting, adding details to the background. Now suggest that they write two sentences to fill in the text, for example: *Here I am at Penzance. I am eating the biggest ice-lolly in the world.* Or *Here I am at Tenby. I am crawling out of my tent in the morning.* (Non-writers should dictate and copy from an adult's script.)

Suggestion(s) for extension

Ask more able children to suggest local places they would like to visit if they were having a holiday at home. These should be places of interest which are not too far away. Ask them to say why they would like to go there and encourage them talk about visits they may have made with their parents.

Suggestion(s) for support

Let children who need support look through a holiday brochure with a friend. Suggest that they choose a place they would like to visit if they could and encourage them to give reasons why. If they find this difficult, ask direct *Why?*

and *What then?* questions to ease the children into finding answers.

Assessment opportunities

Note the children who can give clear reasons for choices, using connective words such as *because* and *so*. The repetition and elaboration part of the activity gives opportunities for assessing the quality of listening.

Display ideas

Outline four suitcase shapes on backing sheets. Give one to each group. Let the children paint and cut out clothes and toys appropriate to their imaginary destinations, then glue these collage-style into the 'suitcases'.

Other aspects of the English PoS covered

Reading – 1b, c.
Writing – 1b.

Reference to the photocopiable sheet

Page 150 provides two empty 'frames' for children to draw their own 'holiday photographs' and complete the text in their own way.

IF...

To encourage children to predict outcomes and explore the possibilities of unusual situations.

†† *Whole class, followed by groups of five or six.*

🕐 *25 minutes.*

Previous skills/knowledge needed

The children need to be able to recognise out-of-the-ordinary situations or circumstances.

Key background information

This activity encourages children to look for reasons that might explain people's unusual behaviour. For example, why would you wear your coat in the classroom? *Perhaps it's because you feel cold. Perhaps you are coming down with 'flu. Perhaps the heating has broken down.* This activity requires some imagination on your part.

Preparation

Arrange to bring in some ordinary things which look out of place inside school, for example: an opened umbrella, a sleeping bag, an alarm clock, pots and pans. Bring in some kitchen gadgets whose use is reasonably obvious.

Resources needed

A few props (as suggested above), one copy per child of photocopiable sheet 151. One copy per child of the photocopiable summative assessment sheet on page 152 (if required).

What to do

Gather the children around you. Show them an unopened umbrella (for instance) and discuss when you use it and what for. Ask if they can think when, if ever, it might be sensible to put an umbrella up inside the school: *If the rain is coming through the ceiling. If the wind has blown the roof off the school. If there is no roof and the sun gets too hot.*

Produce an alarm clock (for instance). Let the children hear the alarm. Talk about clocks and watches in general. Talk about what is special about an alarm clock, when they are used and why they are useful. Let children make suggestions about why you might bring one into school: *If you wanted to have plenty of time to get ready for PE. If you had to remember to give someone their medicine at a particular time. If someone had to feed the guinea-pig before break time.* The children soon get into the swing of answering in this way and make lots of imaginative suggestions.

Show the children some kitchen gadgets (see 'Preparation') and ask where they are usually kept. Ask them to think of reasons why you might bring them into school: *If we needed them for the school play. If we were doing some baking in school. If your kitchen at home were flooded and you needed to have tea in school.*

Go on to discussing what happens if people need help and there is nobody around. What is the special number you can dial on the telephone? Encourage the children to use their knowledge about making 999 calls. Get them to explain how they would go about doing this: what would they say? Discuss with them what might happen to make dialling 999 necessary. Encourage them to think up and describe as many scenarios as possible: *If the house were on fire. If my Mum got ill. If someone went off with my new bike.* This part of the activity gives rise to a number of individual accounts. Encourage the children to listen with attention and concentration, so that they can ask relevant questions of the speaker.

Divide the children into groups. Give each child a copy of photocopiable page 151 and give the groups five minutes to think about what has happened in each of the pictures. (You might set the alarm for this!) When they reassemble, finish off the activity by listening to and discussing their explanations.

Suggestion(s) for extension
Ask more able children to invent and talk through a possible 999 scenario.

Suggestion(s) for support
Work with two or three children. Use the photocopiable sheet and help them to reason out why, for example, a man looks as though he is fishing down the chimney. Go through rational explanations, such as sweeping the chimney. A burglar on Christmas morning? Get them to think about what is on the end of the rope, what is happening at the bottom of the chimney and so on.

Assessment opportunities
This activity can be used for summative assessment, and photocopiable sheet 152 is provided for this purpose. Note the children who can think first of rational explanations and

to make up a narrative around each of the scenarios in the pictures from the photocopiable sheet, or to follow through a 999 story. Use a page for each scene. The children can draw speech bubbles, comic-style, on each page.

Reference to photocopiable sheets

Photocopiable sheet 151 shows four unlikely situations which the children have to explain, using a mixture of practical reasoning and imaginative speculation. Photocopiable sheet 152 can be used for summative assessment of the children's skills in reasoning and speculation, based on this activity.

Performance ideas

The children can make up short drama pieces based on their 999 ideas and use simple hats to indicate which service they have called. Each 'story' could be performed to other classes in the school; possibly at assembly as part of a 'People who help us' project.

who can put over their ideas with confidence. The activity has a further dimension: allowing children to give rein to their imaginations. Listen for those who can cope with the more surreal *If...* ideas and who have appropriate language at their command. Listen for evidence (in the relevance and appropriateness of their responses) that the children have listened carefully.

Opportunities for IT

The children could write out the explanations for the different scenarios using a word processor. Their work could be printed out and stuck next to the various scenario pictures.

Display ideas

This activity is ideal for display in zigzag format. Make the pages large enough to pin on the wall and ask the children

ODD ONE OUT

To help children to make simple deductions through discussing possibilities and clarifying their ideas in words.

†† *Whole class, followed by groups of five or six.*
🕐 *25 minutes.*

Previous skills/knowledge needed

The children need to understand the meaning of *'same'* and *'different'*. It is useful, but not essential, if they have experience of making sets.

Key background information

This activity relies on children being aware of similarities and differences. They must be able to move things around (literally

Reasoning and speculating

or in their imagination), so that they see how perceptions can alter with circumstances: often it is not simply a matter of seeing an object itself as part of a main set (for example, an orange as a fruit) but of seeing how colour, texture and other factors such as shape, can be taken into account. (Cars, lorries, trains and boats are all means of transport, but the boat can be seen as the odd one out because it has no wheels.)

Preparation

Gather together as many different sets of objects as possible: shells, stones, books, toys, fruit – adding a few 'outsiders', such as a carrot, to go among the fruits; a video to make an odd one out among the books.

Resources needed

A variety of sets as suggested above (picture sets could be included, such as *animals* and *transport*), large PE hoops (one for each group), magazines.

What to do

Gather the children together in the story corner. Invite two girls and a boy to come and stand beside you. Tell the children that you are going to play the 'odd one out' game. Can they say who is the odd one out among the three children? Get them to explain why they chose the boy. Still with the same three children, find another way to pair them – for example, John and Julie can go together and Susan becomes the odd one out. Try other variations.

Now work with the fruit set, including, for example, an apple, a banana, an orange and a lemon. Put them in a PE hoop. Ask the children what is the same about all these things. *They are all fruit.* Then they should consider what makes them different: *their skin, shape, taste.* Put the lemon, the orange and the banana together. Can they find the odd one out now? *(It must be the orange: the other two are both yellow. Or it must be the banana: the other two are both more or less round.)* Put all the fruit and a carrot into the hoop. Ask them to find the odd one out now.

Encourage the children to talk through the 'same and different' discoveries. Ask them to move things around and set puzzles for the other children, perhaps placing the carrot

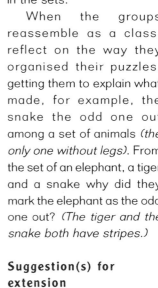

and the orange in the hoop, so that colour becomes the criterion and anything that is not orange becomes the odd one out.

Give practice with other kinds of set, always making sure that the children are able to think through and articulate the reasons for their 'odd one out' decisions.

Divide the children into groups. Give each group a hoop and loosely connected sets of either artefacts or pictures. Give them a set time to make a 'puzzle' for the other groups, who must then find the odd one(s) out in the sets.

When the groups reassemble as a class, reflect on the way they organised their puzzles, getting them to explain what made, for example, the snake the odd one out among a set of animals *(the only one without legs)*. From the set of an elephant, a tiger and a snake why did they mark the elephant as the odd one out? *(The tiger and the snake both have stripes.)*

Suggestion(s) for extension

This time use two hoops. Put shells and stones on the floor. Choose two children to sort the objects into the hoops, shells in one, stones in the other. Show that by linking the hoops, all the white objects (both shells and stones) can be grouped together. Ask the children to think about other ways to organise things into the link, for example, by shape or by texture. Ask them to explain the thinking behind their reorganisation.

Suggestion(s) for support

Give these children no more than three or four objects to work with, perhaps three books and a video or three balls and a teddy bear. Get them to find and talk about the odd one out.

Assessment opportunities

Listen to the children talking about their conclusions. Can they give a coherent explanation for what makes one object an odd one out? Can they move from one criterion to another?

SPEAKING AND LISTENING

NEXT?

To help children to use a picture-based context to speculate about and discuss ways in which a story will end.

†† *Whole class, followed by small-group work.*

🕐 *20 minutes.*

Previous skills/knowledge needed
Experience of listening to stories and looking at picture books.

Key background information
Children should be encouraged to think about how stories end. Create an interest in this idea by occasionally pausing in story-telling or story-reading to discuss what will make a good or a funny ending. The children should be made aware that there is more than one good way to finish a story – different people will have different, but equally valid, ideas.

Display ideas
Make a frieze of large overlapping hoops. Get the children to paint and cut out from magazines fruit and vegetables, shells and stones and different kinds of toys. These can then be stuck on to the wall frieze in linked sets.

Preparation
Copy and enlarge photocopiable sheet 153. Cut it into sections, so that the children can sequence the pictures into a story format.

Resources needed
Enlarged copies of photocopiable sheet 153 (one per child), a flip chart or whiteboard, a selection of picture story-books from the class library, coloured pencils.

Performance ideas
Get the children to present an 'Odd one out' show. Go from something relatively obvious, such as one boy with four girls, to a more difficult case such as six children, only one of whom is wearing one shoe or odd socks. The 'audience' must try to spot the odd one out.

What to do
Gather the children in the story corner. Open one of the picture books and read it almost to the end. Pause, as

Other aspects of the English PoS covered
Reading – 2c.
Writing – 1c.

SPEAKING AND LISTENING

suggested above, and discuss possible endings with the children. For example, if you have used *Where the Wild Things Are* by Maurice Sendak, ask how else Max might have got home: by helicopter? by hot air balloon? on a magic carpet? What would have happened if Mum had been out when Max got back? What would Dad or Grandma or Uncle Philip have said to him? What would have happened if he had turned up at school with the Wild Things?

Now spread out the pictures cut from photocopiable sheet 153. Encourage the children to put them into the correct sequence, and then tell the story as far as they can from the picture sequence. They should name the children and the dog. Then pose the question: *What happens next?* Remind them that it is not necessarily what they themselves might do, but what would make a good story. Perhaps the children rescue the dog and take it home. How would they do this? Do they get their clothes wet? What does mum say?

Ask the children to think of a sad, exciting or funny ending (for instance, just as they reach the dog it gets out of the river, soaking the children as it shakes itself and ambles off – in the opposite direction, no longer needing to be rescued). Scribe some of the possibilities on the flip chart.

Let the children break into groups, each to come up with its own preferred ending to the story. After discussion, the members of the group should work as individuals, each drawing the ending which their group has chosen in the blank box on their photocopiable sheet. They should colour in the pictures for the rest of the story.

Bring the groups back together and ask them to take turns to tell their own version of the picture story from beginning to end. This may need to be organised well, so that each child in the group has a part to tell.

Suggestion(s) for extension
Children in each group can cut up a comic strip story into individual pictures, omitting the final one. Pass the story to another group, asking *What happens next?* Each group makes up a new ending, then tells the completed story to the others.

Suggestion(s) for support
Use the original storyline and suggest that children work in pairs to find a satisfactory ending. Do not ask the less confident children to retell the whole story: take it as read and ask them to draw the new ending. From the drawing, encourage them to talk to an adult helper about how the story ends.

Assessment opportunities
The children should be using the language of narrative, reasoning and speculating about what will happen next, from the clues in the pictures. When describing what takes place in the final episode of the story, note the children's use of logical phrases such as, *and then ..., so they had to ..., but they couldn't, so ..., then next they ...* and so on.

Display ideas
Copy the comic-strip style and ask the children (in groups) to paint their own (much enlarged) version of each separate section of the story, so that each section is painted by one

What happens next?

group. From the children's dictation, scribe a précis beneath each picture and mount as a wall story.

Other aspects of the English PoS covered
Reading – 1c; 2c.
Writing – 1c; 2b, 3.

Reference to photocopiable sheet
The correct sequence into which children should arrange the pictures is: *1. Children waving goodbye to Mum. 2. Children*

walking along river path. 3. They see bullies tugging dog along by its lead. 4. Dog falls into river. 5. Bullies run off. 6. Blank picture (for child to draw what happens next).

Performance ideas
Give each group a starter picture from which to make up a new story as an unfolding drama. Once they are happy with the sequence of events, let them perform the story to the others in the class. It might be possible to stop the action and let the audience guess how the story will end. Take a variety of answers, then restart the play to see who, if anyone, was correct.

FEATHERS IN THE SKY

To encourage children to use predictive language.

†† *Whole class.*

⏲ *20 minutes.*

Previous knowledge needed
Experience of natural events and a general understanding of the difference between fantasy and reality.

Key background information
This activity relies on the children's understanding of the unlikely nature of the situations posed, for example: *What if it snowed feathers?* They have to make an imaginative leap to consider possible answers to the *What if ...?* questions. Encourage the children to reason out ways of coping with strange events, what things would look like, what they (and others) would do *if ...*

SPEAKING AND LISTENING

Preparation

Photocopy resource pages 154 and 155 and cut each copy into two separate pictures, ready for distribution.

Resources needed

A flip chart, coloured pencils, a cap with a badge (such as a traffic warden's hat), one copy per child of each of photocopiable sheets 154 and 155 (each sheet cut into two separate pictures).

What to do

Get the children sitting together, as if ready to listen to a story. Say that they are going to have a new and important job – as problem-solvers! A problem-solver must think of good ways out of a difficulty, and to help them you have a special hat for them to wear when their turn comes along. Show the children the hat with the badge to demonstrate just how important the job is.

Ask the children to close their eyes and think of a very snowy day, the snowiest day they can remember. Tell them that there is something very different about the snow today – it's all made of feathers. The Town Council needs to call the problem-solvers in.

When they have opened their eyes again, discuss with the children what would be different about feathers instead of snowflakes. *They won't melt away. They will be very soft and dry to lie on. You can't make snowballs with them.*

Give out copies of the appropriate picture from photocopiable sheet 154. Go on to say: *So here we are with the streets covered in feathers. Who would like to help solve the first problem – how do we clear them away?* When

the hands go up, choose a child to have first go. Let her wear the hat. *I think we will need to brush the feathers away.* Ask the others if they think this idea would work. Why not? *Feathers are too light. They would just blow away. The feathers would make you sneeze.* Give another child the chance to be an official problem-solver.

Encourage the children's conversation/argument to flow from problem-solver and back again to the class. Try to orchestrate the discussion so that everyone with a point of view/question can put it to the child in the 'hot seat'.

Pose a new problem. *What would happen if a dragon came to tea?* (Give out copies of the appropriate picture from photocopiable sheet 154, to stimulate discussion.) The problem-solver should think of the size of the creature, what he would say to make Mum enthusiastic about the visit, what the dragon might like to eat, what they should do in the event of the dragon breathing fire and so on. Keep the problem-solving going at a fast and furious pace, with the hat being passed on to a new wearer whenever the problem-solver gets stuck.

Introduce further *What if ...* scenarios. *What if it rained pink ink? What if shoes grew on trees? What if the roof blew off the school? What if a Martian arrived at school? (Where would he park his spaceship? How would we manage to talk to him? What would we tell Mum when we got home?)*

After 20 minutes or so, bring the discussions to an end. Let the children examine the other two pictures, cut from photocopiable sheet 155. Encourage them to explore these pictures and to discuss (informally) how they would deal with the problems implied by these situations. Finally, they could colour in all four pictures.

Assessment opportunities

Note the children who are/are not capable of using predictive thought and language – for example, *If it snowed feathers then... It would be hard to make a snowman... The trees would look as though they had wings...* and so on. Those who cannot use predictive language in an imaginative way may say something like: *If it snowed feathers it would be very funny. If it snowed feathers it wouldn't be real.* This kind of answer indicates that children have missed the point of the activity, and need further practice in making an 'imaginative leap'.

Suggestion(s) for extension

With the children working in pairs, ask one child to imagine a new *What if...?* possibility and the other to act as problem-solver. They can change places once a solution has been suggested. Ask them to draw pictures of, and write stories about, the situations they come up with.

Suggestion(s) for support

If possible, work on this activity with a small group. Use the photocopiable sheets and discuss with them what is happening in each picture. Ask specific questions, so that the children are thinking about only one possibility at a time, for example: *Has a dragon ever come to your house? Do you think it would be able to get in the front door? Why not? What do you think he might like for his tea? What would your Mum say about it, do you think?*

Display ideas

Divide the class into groups and give each one a different *What if...?* idea to work on. Using A3 size sugar paper, get them to make up a page for a floor book. The page can be divided into four sections, with a different consequence illustrated in each section. (See illustration.) Title the page, for example, *What if a dragon came to tea?* finally stapling the pages together in a cover as a class book. (You may find that a spiral binding makes a more durable book.)

Other aspects of the English PoS covered

Reading – 2c.
Writing – 1c; 2a, b.

Reference to photocopiable sheets

Photocopiable sheets 154 and 155 show four situations which are not only unlikely, but require explanations involving a fantastic or speculative element. The children are asked to deal with these situations practically, as if they were realistic problems.

Performance ideas

The children could make each of the unlikely situations into a short drama piece, including a 'practical' resolution.

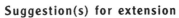

WHAT'S IN GRANDMA'S PARCEL?

To help children to use elimination and prediction techniques to develop and clarify their ideas.

†† *Whole class.*

⏱ *20 minutes.*

Previous skills/knowledge needed

Some experience in estimating weights informally, for example: *I think the brick is heavier than my reading book... My pencil is lighter than my lunch box.*

Key background information

This activity works best when the children are encouraged to combine reasoning with an imaginative leap. Help them towards making quite outrageous suggestions which add a touch of humour to the proceedings, for example: *It can't be a live dinosaur. Why not? They don't exist any more!*

Preparation

Make up a number of parcels, wrapped in fancy paper for best effect, first hiding them in a bin liner. Try to provide a range of shapes and sizes, so that there is a very small, very heavy parcel; a large, light parcel; something round; something that says *Fragile, handle with care* and so on. Work on the basis of question and answer, asking first what is *not* in the parcel, then asking why they think it is not a particular thing (see above).

Resources needed

Parcels (as suggested above), different kinds of wrapping paper (birthday, Christmas, new baby), sticky tape, string, a selection of 'presents' (toys, books, rolled-up maps), a bin liner, a flip chart, one copy per child of photocopiable sheet 156 (for support only).

What to do

Keep the parcels well hidden in the bin liner and gather the children in the story corner. Initiate a discussion about postal delivery and receiving parcels through the post. *Who sends you parcels? When? What do you do when it's your birthday and the postwoman rings the bell?* and so on. Talk about the element of surprise in receiving and opening a present. Talk about the best present that Grandma or Grandad might send for Christmas, birthday – or just as a complete surprise!

Tell the children that you are going to play a guessing game with surprises you have hidden in the black bag. Build up a feeling of excitement and interest – all eyes will be upon you as you produce the first well-wrapped parcel. Talk about what the children can deduce from simply looking at the parcel. If it is wrapped in brown paper with stamps on it, it will have come through the post. If the wrapping paper has *Happy Birthday* on it, it must be for someone's birthday.

Now ask them to look at the shape of the parcel. Encourage them to guess what *can't* be inside – *It's not a doll's house. Why? It isn't big enough/It's the wrong shape/ It's got a label that says 'Love to Uncle John' on it.* Scribe all the 'can't be' answers on the flip chart, and encourage zany ideas.

113

Next give the children a chance to feel how heavy the parcel is, to explore the shape with their fingers and to look closely at the wrapping for clues. Get them to think about what could be small, spiky and heavy that Uncle John might like for his birthday – a brass hedgehog? Ask one of the children to open the parcel to see who has made the best guess.

Go through a similar process for the other parcels. Always encourage the children to express their reasons for and against a particular guess. If there is a disagreement among the children, encourage them to listen to others with courtesy, then to express their own ideas without heat.

Suggestion(s) for extension

When the children have played the guessing game *What's in Grandma's parcel?*, arrange them in groups and ask them to choose from among your set of 'presents', for example, something suitable for a new baby, then to wrap it in 'new baby' paper; or a present that Mum might like for her birthday, and so on. Each group should have a different 'present' to wrap and a sheet of suitable wrapping paper. (They might design their own paper – see 'Display ideas'). They should then exchange parcels with another group and try to guess the contents.

Suggestion(s) for support

Use photocopiable page 156 for the children who need support. Ask them to draw a present which would fit inside each parcel outline (for example: a football in the round parcel, a book in the rectangular one). Help them to write the labels. Encourage them to talk about why they chose a particular 'present' to fit into each parcel. Ask questions about what things would not be suitable, and again encourage them to give reasons.

What's in Grandma's parcel?

Assessment opportunities

This activity provides ample opportunity to assess the way children express their reasons for and against certain possibilities, for example: *It can't be... because... I don't think that's right because... It isn't heavy enough... It isn't the right shape to be...* and so on. Note those children who have this clarity of reasoning and the means to express it.

Display ideas

After discussing and looking at a variety of wrapping papers for different occasions, ask the children to design their own. Use potato cuts or spatter-paint techniques to make patterns

and get them to print the logo *(Happy Christmas, Welcome to the new baby)* in felt-tipped pen after the patterns have dried. Display the finished designs on the wall.

If it is near Christmas, make collage cut-outs of the Kings bringing gifts to the baby Jesus. Make a collage of brightly wrapped presents beneath a cut-out Christmas tree. The shapes of the parcels could suggest their contents.

Other aspects of the English PoS covered
Writing – 1c.

Reference to photocopiable sheet
Photocopiable sheet 156 is used as a resource for a support activity (see above), reinforcing the children's awareness of the shapes and uses of objects.

WHO USES WHAT?

To encourage children to make tentative decisions through sorting and matching, and to evaluate and discuss their conclusions.

†† *Whole class, followed by groups of four or five.*

🕐 *20 minutes.*

Previous skills/knowledge needed
Experience of looking at picture books and talking about the illustrations.

Key background information
This activity is a matching exercise which encourages children to look carefully at pictures, to think about how objects are used and to reason out connections. There will, therefore, be some lively discussion, so the usual rules of speaking and listening must be observed. (See the Introduction to the book on page 8.) Make sure that the children listen carefully to each other, so that they can remember the key points of an argument and be ready to present their own deductions and points of view.

Preparation
Make one enlarged copy of photocopiable sheet 157 and cut out the pictures. Photocopy the sheet onto card and cut up to make a matching game. (You will need one set for each group.) Bring in some real objects for the children to handle (see below).

Resources needed
Copies of photocopiable page 157, as above; a set of objects which a nurse might use, such as bandages, empty pill bottles, small scissors; objects which a teacher might use, such as chalk, red pen, gummed stars; flowerpots, trowel, seed packets for the gardener; screwdriver, hammer, nails for the carpenter; PE hoops.

What to do
Sit the children comfortably in the story corner. Begin with a discussion on what they would like to do when they grow up, encouraging the children to express themselves confidently and clearly. Ask for reasons for their choices and encourage them to think about some of the realities of the job, for example, some of the routine parts of what a model or a footballer actually does.

Show the enlarged pictures of the nurse, teacher, gardener and carpenter. Ask if they can guess what these people do. What clues do they see in the picture? (Uniform,

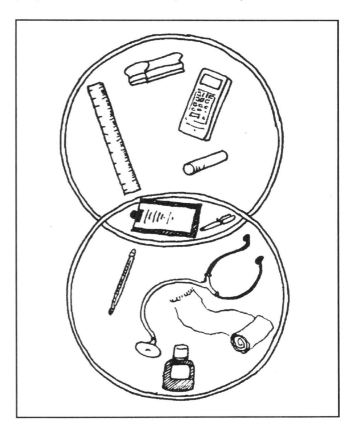

chalk, dirty hands, tool box.) Suggest that they search the background for more clues. What other job might the teacher have? She doesn't wear a uniform. Who else might get their hands dirty when they are working? and so on. Always try to move the discussion forward, encouraging the children to make deductions and connections.

Space out four hoops on the floor. Put a picture in each. Then bring out the real 'tools of the trade' one by one, asking first what each is, what it is used for and finally who might use it. Ask a child to place the object in the appropriate hoop.

Encourage discussion of objects which might be used by more than one person. A clipboard and pen, for example, might be used by the nurse and by the teacher, so overlap the hoops as shown. (See illustration above.)

Divide the children into groups of four or five, and give each group a set of cards made from the photocopiable sheet. Ask them to match objects to trades. Give the groups blank cards and ask them to draw some more objects which teachers, nurses, gardeners and carpenters might use.

Bring the children back into the whole-class group and ask them to share their ideas for the extra 'tools', explaining what they are used for and why they have suggested them.

Suggestion(s) for extension

Find some newspaper photographs of, for example, oil-rig workers, librarians, ambulance crews and police constables, and ask the children to discuss what objects these people might use in their jobs. Ask them to draw picture cards of the objects to go with the newspaper photographs. They might mount the pictures to make a new *Who Uses What?* game. They can then introduce this new game to the rest of the class.

Suggestion(s) for support

The children can work in pairs, a confident child with one who is less so. Ask them to match the objects and pictures, using the hoops. Get the less confident children to tell you why they have arranged things in the way they have. Let them colour in the pictures on the photocopiable sheet to consolidate their sense of how the elements are related.

Assessment opportunities

Listen for the language of reasoned argument: *This is why we... I think a nurse/gardener might use...*

Display ideas

Ask the children to paint a large portrait of each worker and place this in the middle of a circular frieze; then paint and cut out pictures of the things the worker might use in her or his job, pasting these around the central image. (See illustration.)

Make a large class book for each worker depicted on the photocopiable sheet, with the children either writing or dictating to an adult scribe and then copying sentences under pictures of the things the worker uses in her or his job. Follow this with making books about what the children want to do when they grow up.

Other aspects of the English PoS covered

Writing – 1b, c; 2e.

Reference to photocopiable sheet

Photocopiable sheet 157 is a resource for a matching game in which the children decide – and explain – which person would use which object in their work.

Photocopiables

The pages in this section can be photocopied for use in the classroom or school which has purchased this book, and do not need to be declared in any return in respect of any photocopying licence.

They comprise a varied selection of both pupil and teacher resources, including pupil worksheets, resource material and record sheets to be completed by the teacher or children. Each photocopiable sheet is related to an individual activity in the book; the name of the activity is indicated at the top of the sheet, together with a page reference indicating where the lesson plan for that activity can be found.

Individual pages are discussed in detail within each lesson plan, accompanied by ideas for adaptation where appropriate – of course, each sheet can be adapted to suit your own needs and those of your class. Sheets can also be coloured, laminated, mounted on to card, enlarged and so on where appropriate.

Pupil worksheets and record sheets have spaces provided for children's names and for noting the date on which each sheet was used. This means that, if so required, they can be included easily within any pupil assessment portfolio. Photocopiable sheets 120, 130, 134, 138, 145 and 152 are intended to be used for summative assessment, and accompany the activities (one per chapter) designated for this purpose.

Nursery rhymes self-assessment sheet

Name _____   Date _____

Can you do these things:

> **1**. Find the correct last word left off a rhyme? ☐

> **2**. Say a whole line aloud in the right place? ☐

> **3**. Make up the start of a new rhyme, replacing the name in the rhyme with your own name or a friend's name? ☐

> **4**. Make up a new line to complete an unfinished rhyme, based on one you know? ☐

▲ Tick the box for each thing you have done.

The lamb was sure to

~~run~~
bounce
climb

Nursery rhymes

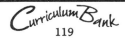

SPEAKING AND
LISTENING

Traditional stories, see page 21

Storytelling and performance

Name: _____ Age: _____

Class: _____ Date of assessment: _____

Comments on ability in storytelling and performance:	
Can talk to the teacher or other adult with confidence.	
Can speak with an awareness of Standard English.	
Can listen to a story with attention and understanding.	
Can take turns to speak and listen.	
Can recall details of a story he/she has heard.	
Can think logically about the sequence of events.	
Can retell the story in her/his own words.	
Can join in the repetitive words or phrases of a traditional story.	

1 Working towards target. **2** Making good progress.
3 Has achieved target level.

General comments:

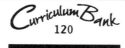

SPEAKING AND
LISTENING

Alice had an angry alligator, see page 24

Alice had an alphabet

Name _____   Date _____

b	s	r	o
e	t	f	d
g	m	n	j
k	a	w	z
v	p	h	u
i	y	l	c

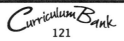

Day and night, see page 25

Day and night

Name _____   Date _____

day

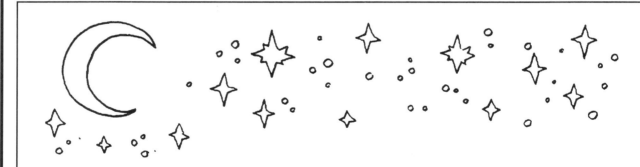

night

SPEAKING AND
LISTENING

Magic fruit tree, see page 33

Magic fruit

Name _____ Date _____

pear

cherries

orange

apple

SPEAKING AND
LISTENING

Message in a bottle, see page 34

Message in a bottle

Date

Name

SPEAKING AND
LISTENING

Once I met a monster, see page 36

Here comes the monster

Name _____   Date _____

**SPEAKING AND
LISTENING**

One blue butterfly, see page 38

One blue butterfly

Name _____

Date _____

10	6
9	7
8	8
3	—
4	2
5	1

SPEAKING AND LISTENING

Sounds of silence

Name _____   Date _____

Silence is...

Silence is...

Silence is...

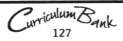

SPEAKING AND LISTENING

The senses, see page 42

The senses

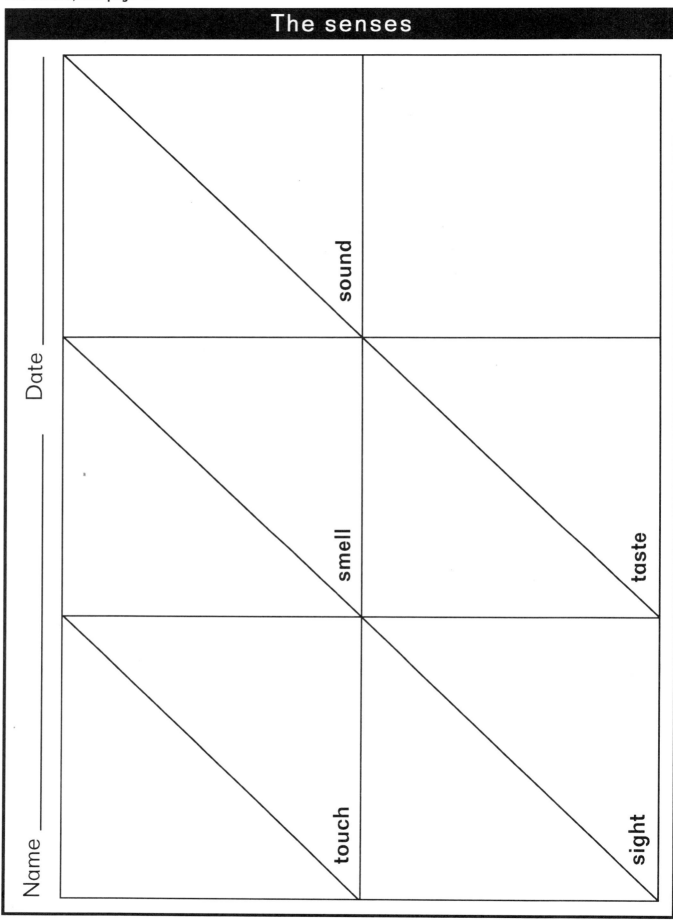

Date

Name

The sun, see page 46

The sun

Date _____

Name _____

sun

SPEAKING AND LISTENING

Extending vocabulary

Name: _____   Age: _____

Class: _____   Date of assessment: _____

Comments on ability in use of vocabulary:	
Can talk to the teacher or other adult with confidence.	
Can speak with an awareness of Standard English.	
Can listen to others with attention and understanding.	
Can take turns to speak and listen.	
Can use vocabulary that is appropriate, broad and interesting.	
Can use similes and make comparisons effectively.	
Can use imaginative language effectively.	
Can make observations using the language of the senses.	

1 Working towards target. **2** Making good progress.
3 Has achieved target level.

General comments:

SPEAKING AND LISTENING

Framed!

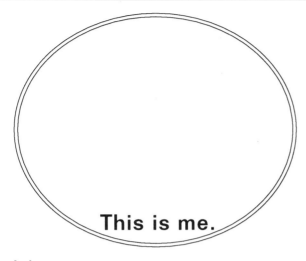

This is me.

My name is _____

I am _____ years old.

My address is _____

_____

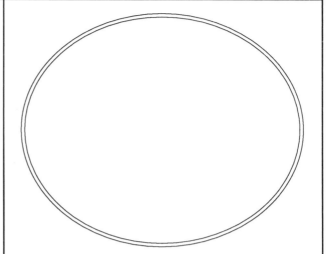

This is _____

_____ is my _____

and is _____ years old.

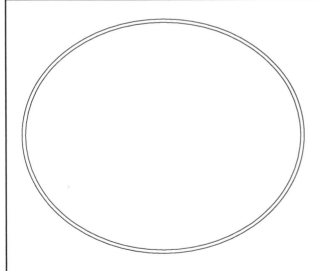

This is _____

_____ is my _____

and is _____ years old.

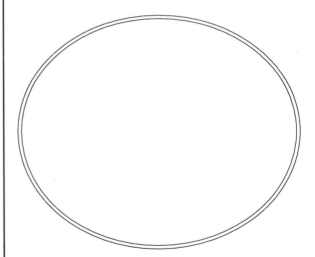

This is _____

_____ is my _____

and is _____ years old.

SPEAKING AND LISTENING

Harry Egg's hair, see page 54

Harry Egg's hair

Name _____   Date _____

Different hats, see page 57

Different hats

Name _____ Date _____

SPEAKING AND
LISTENING

Information handling

Name: _____   Age: _____

Class: _____   Date of assessment: _____

Comments on ability in handling information:	
Can work effectively with other children.	
Can talk to the teacher or other adult with confidence.	
Can speak with an awareness of Standard English.	
Can take turns to speak and listen.	
Can present simple factual information in an organised way.	
Can listen to and interpret spoken information.	
Can offer relevant descriptions based on observation.	

1 Working towards target. **2** Making good progress.
3 Has achieved target level.

General comments:

Teddy bears' picnic, see page 61

Teddy bears' picnic

Makes about 30 biscuits.

Ingredients:
225g (8oz) cooking chocolate
500g (1lb 2oz) fruit and nut muesli

You will need:
paper cases, saucepan, bowl, baking tray.

This recipe needs adult supervision.

Chocolate muesli crunch

Break up the chocolate. Melt it in a bowl held over a saucepan of hot water. Remove from heat and leave to cool for a few minutes.

Stir in some muesli, until the mixture is just held together by the chocolate. Spoon the mixture into small paper cases and leave on a baking tray to cool, then refrigerate until set.

Makes about 30 sweets.

Ingredients:
1 egg white
360g (12oz) icing sugar
a few drops vanilla essence (or other flavouring)

You will need:
a board, a whisk, a bowl, a knife (not too sharp), a wooden spoon.

Vanilla creams

Whisk the egg white until frothy. Sieve the icing sugar to remove lumps. Using the wooden spoon, gradually beat about two-thirds of the icing sugar (a bit at a time) into the egg white. Add vanilla essence to taste (do not use too much, or it will taste horrible).

Spoon the mixture onto a board and knead in the rest of the icing sugar. Divide the mixture in half and shape each half into a long cylinder. Chop into roughly half a centimetre thick slices. Roll each slice into a ball. Leave to set in the refrigerator.

SPEAKING AND LISTENING

The face in the mirror

Name _____   Date _____

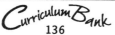

Detectives

Name _____   Date _____

soft	**bumpy**
hairy	**shiny**
rough	**hard**

**SPEAKING AND
LISTENING**

How does it work? see page 73

Explaining and understanding

Name: _____ Age: _____

Class: _____ Date of assessment: _____

Comments on ability in explaining and understanding:	
Can work effectively with other children.	
Can talk to the teacher or other adult with confidence.	
Can speak with an awareness of Standard English.	
Can listen to others with attention and understanding.	
Can take turns to speak and listen.	
Can respond appropriately to instruction and explanation.	
Can explain a process to others using fluent clear language.	
Can use accurate descriptive language.	

1 Working towards target. 2 Making good progress.
3 Has achieved target level.

General comments:

SPEAKING AND LISTENING

What's happening? see page 75

What's happening here? (1)

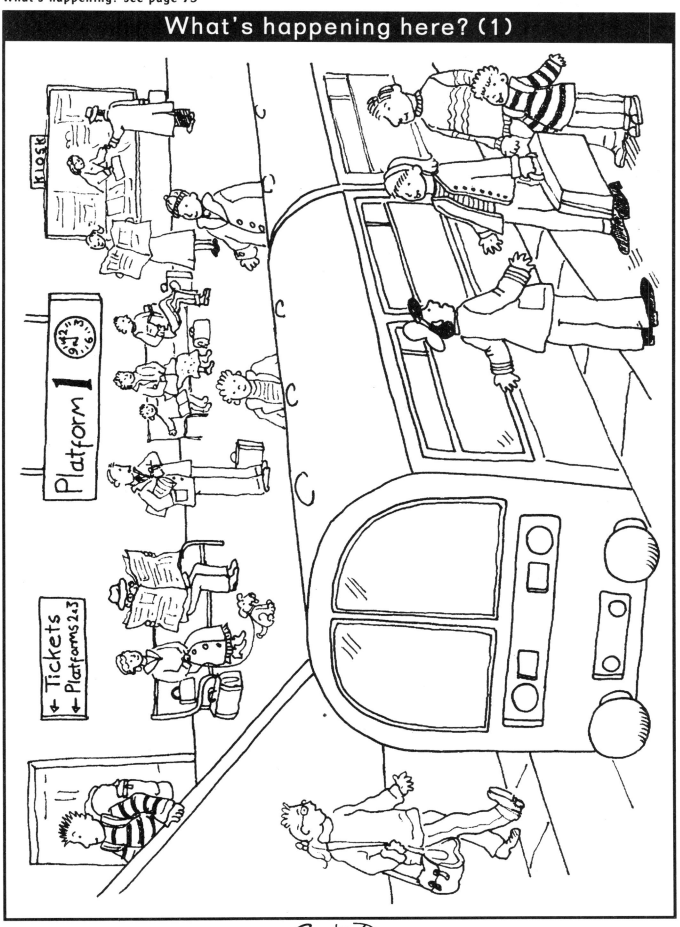

What's happening? see page 75

What's happening here? (2)

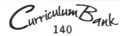

SPEAKING AND
LISTENING

Why? Why? Why?

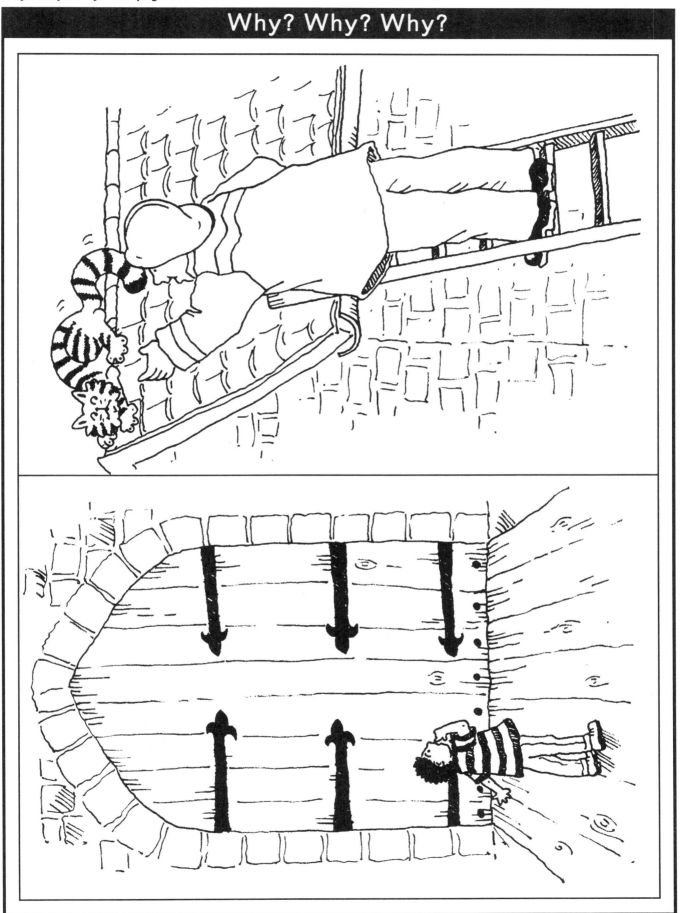

You'll like our school

Name _____   Date _____

Our school is called _____	Our headteacher is called _____
Our class teacher is called _____	Our caretaker is called _____
Our school cook is called _____	My favourite part of the school is _____

Paint your dragon, see page 87

Dragon colours

Name _____   Date _____

I feel blue, see page 89

I feel blue

Name _____ Date _____

SPEAKING AND
LISTENING

Litterbugs, see page 91

Opinion and persuasion

Name: _____ Age: _____

Class: _____ Date of assessment: _____

Comments on ability in expressing opinion and persuading:	
Can work effectively with other children.	
Can talk to the teacher and other adults with confidence.	
Can speak with an awareness of Standard English.	
Can listen to others with attention and understanding.	
Can take turns to speak and listen.	
Can put forward a point of view with confidence.	
Can use the language of persuasion effectively.	
Can articulate thoughts and feelings.	

1 Working towards target. **2** Making good progress.
3 Has achieved target level.

General comments:

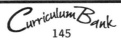

SPEAKING AND LISTENING

The best pets, see page 93

The best pets

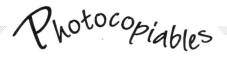
My imaginary pet

Name _____   Date _____

My imaginary pet is a _____

It is called _____

I like it because _____

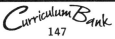
SPEAKING AND LISTENING

What have you done? see page 97

What have you done?

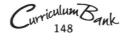

The whole picture, see page 100

The whole picture

Name _____   Date _____

FARM FRESH VEGETABLES

SPEAKING AND LISTENING

Photocopiables

Holiday photographs, see page 102

Holiday photographs

Name _____   Date _____

Here I am at _____

I am _____

Curriculum Bank
150

SPEAKING AND LISTENING

If... see page 104

If...

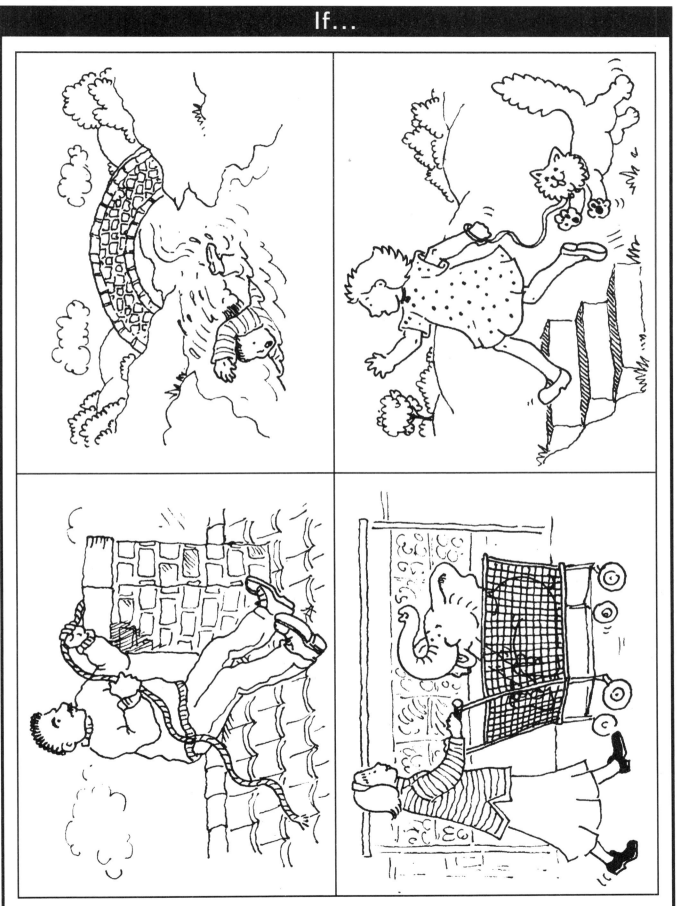

SPEAKING AND
LISTENING

If... see page 104

Reasoning and speculating

Name: _____ Age: _____

Class: _____ Date of assessment: _____

Comments on ability in reasoning and speculating:	
Can work effectively with other children.	
Can talk to the teacher or other adult with confidence.	
Can speak with an awareness of Standard English.	
Can listen to others with attention and understanding.	
Can take turns to speak and listen.	
Can make simple deductions and evaluate them.	
Can interpret a situation in an imaginative way.	

1 Working towards target. **2** Making good progress.
3 Has achieved target level.

General comments:

SPEAKING AND LISTENING

What happens next?

Feathers in the sky, see page 110

Strange problems (1)

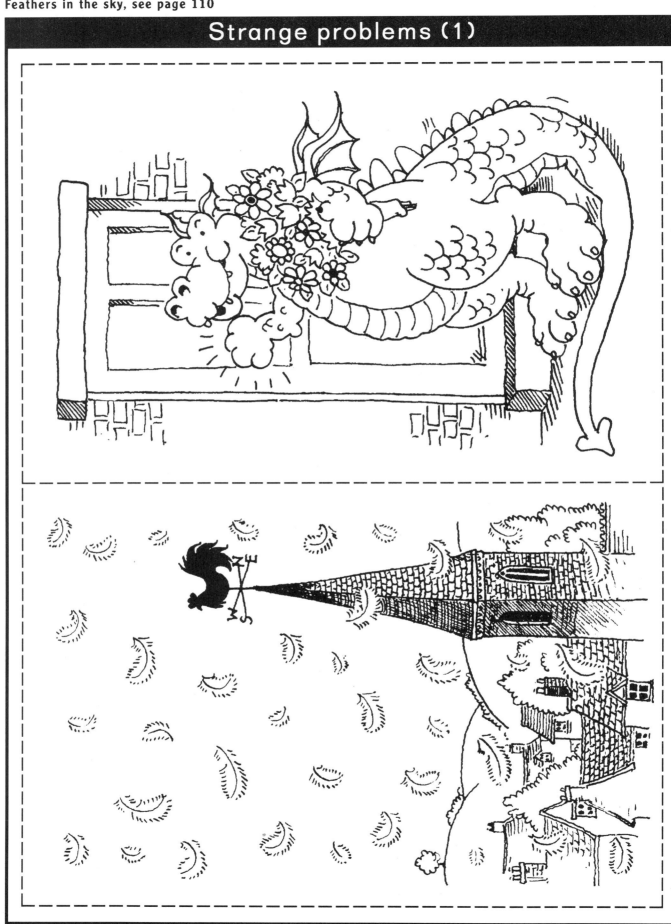

Feathers in the sky, see page 110

Strange problems (2)

SPEAKING AND LISTENING

What's in Grandma's parcel?

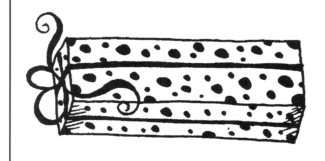

SPEAKING AND LISTENING

Who uses what? see page 115

Who uses what?

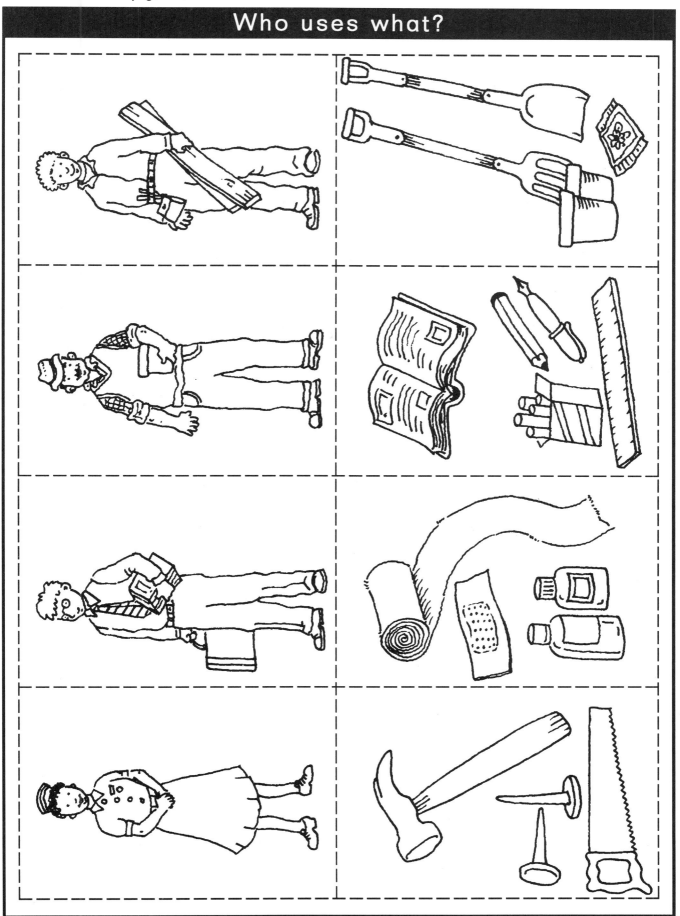

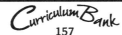

SPEAKING AND
LISTENING

INFORMATION TECHNOLOGY WITHIN SPEAKING AND LISTENING

The information technology outlined in this book can be used to develop and assess children's IT capabilities as outlined in the National Curriculum.

The main focus for development of IT capability within these activities is the communication of specific information through the use of word processing.

Word processing

Although the key aspect of this Curriculum Bank is speaking and listening, many of the suggested activities can lead to some form of writing. Many of the display suggestions contain ideas for scribing or simple writing activities, which could be carried out at the computer using a word processor or simple desk-top publishing package. However, teachers will need to make sure that any use of the computer does not detract from the main purpose of the activity.

Of course, not every child in the class has to undertake every writing task suggested in the activities. The teacher could organise children to undertake different writing tasks over a term or a year, some using traditional writing methods and others using the computer. This would also give teachers an opportunity to provide activities at different levels

of IT capability, and to discuss with different children the relative merits of different uses of IT.

During Key Stage 1, pupils will be developing their confidence and competence in using the standard computer keyboard. They should be taught a range of basic keyboard and word-processing skills. These should include:

▲ an understanding of the layout of the keyboard and where the letter and number keys are found;

▲ how to make capital letters and characters found above the number keys using the shift key;

▲ how to use the delete key to erase words and letters;

▲ how to use the cursor/arrow keys or the mouse to position the cursor at the desired position;

▲ the use of more than a single finger/hand when typing, particularly as they become more proficient and know where letters are located;

▲ how to use the space bar, pressing it with their thumbs;

▲ how the word processor will 'wrap' text around the end

of the line, so there is no need to press the return key at the end of each line;

▲ how to join text using the delete key;

▲ how to separate text or create new lines by using the return key;

▲ how to move the cursor to a mistake and correct it, rather than deleting all the text back to the mistake, making the correction and then retyping the deleted text;

▲ how to print out their completed work, initially with support from the teacher, but eventually on their own.

It is important that the children have opportunities to originate their work at the computer keyboard, rather than always writing it out longhand and simply using the word processor to make a 'fair copy' for display purposes.

Young children will take a long time to enter text at the keyboard, so it is important to ensure that the writing tasks are kept short and that (where possible) other support is available to teach and to assist the child's development. Many of the extension or display ideas in this book are ideal for this purpose, as the writing tasks are short and can be shared among a large group or class of children. The children can then make their own individual copies and print them out, or each child's idea or line can be added under the last to make a class poem (as in the 'Alice had an angry alligator' activity on page 24).

If parents or other adults are available to help, their support can often be used in this way – provided that they have the relevant skills and know when to intervene. Alternatively, adult support can be used for scribing longer passages, typing in the children's work and then going through it with them to edit and amend the text.

Children will also need to save their work if they are unable to finish it in one session. They should be taught how to save a file onto a hard or floppy disk, so that eventually they can do this without teacher assistance. They will also need to be shown how to locate and retrieve their work.

Very young writers may benefit from the use of a concept keyboard linked to the word processor. Appropriate overlays can then be produced, with the relevant words and phrases already on them. This is particularly useful for sequencing activities in which children are given instructions.

Framework software such as *My World 2* (SEMERC) can be set up in similar ways, so that collections of words and phrases can be dragged to a writing area, with children adding extra words from the keyboard as they need them.

IT links

The grids on this page relate the activities in this Curriculum Bank to specific areas of IT and to relevant software resources. Activities are referenced by page number; bold page numbers indicate activities which have expanded IT content (in relation to a specific area of IT). The software listed is a selection of programs generally available to primary schools, and is not intended as a recommended list. The software featured should be available from most good educational software retailers.

AREA OF IT	SOFTWARE	ACTIVITIES (PAGE NOS.)					
		CHAP 1	CHAP 2	CHAP 3	CHAP 4	CHAP 5	CHAP 6
Communicating Information	Word processor	14, 21	**24**, 28, 31, 34, 38, 44	**54**, 64	70, 71, 75	89, 91, 93	104
Communicating Information	Concept keyboard	16		54			
Communicating Information	DTP				75	91	
Communicating Information	Art package	14	31, **33**, 36, 38	55, 66		84, 91	
Communicating Information	Multi-media					93	
Information Handling	Branching database						100
Information Handling	Database		**29**				
Information Handling	Graphing software		29			84	
Control	Tape recorder		40	**58**	77		

SOFTWARE TYPE	BBC/MASTER	RISCOS	NIMBUS/186	WINDOWS	MACINTOSH
Word processor	*Stylus* *Folio* *Prompt/Writer*	*Phases* *Pendown* *Desk Top Folio*	*All Write* *Write On* *Caxton Press*	*My Word* *Kid Works 2* *Creative Writer*	*Kid Works 2* *EasyWorks* *Creative Writer*
DTP	*Front Page* *Extra* *Typesetter*	*Desk Top Folio* *1st Page*	*Front Page Extra* *NewSPAper*	*Creative Writer* *NewSPAper*	*Creative Writer*
Art package		*1st Paint* *Kid Pix* *Splash*		*Colour Magic* *Kid Pix 2*	*Kid Pix 2*
Drawing package	*Picture Builder*	*Draw* *Picture IT*	*Picture Builder*		
Authoring		*Hyperstudio* *Rainbow* *Portfolio*		*Hyperstudio* *MM Box*	*Hyperstudio*
Database	*Our Facts* *Grass* *Pigeonhole* *Datashow*	*DataSweet* *Find IT*	*Our Facts* *Datashow*	*Sparks* *Claris Works* *Information Workshop*	*Claris Works* *Easy Works*
Graphing software	*Datashow*	*Pictogram* *Picture Point* *DataSweet*	*Datagraph*	*Datagraph* *Easy Works*	*Easy Works*

SPEAKING AND LISTENING

	MATHS	SCIENCE	HISTORY	GEOGRAPHY	D & T	IT	ART	MUSIC	RE/PSE
STORYTELLING AND PERFORMANCE	Counting activities based on rhymes.	Thinking about plants and birds in the garden.		A story about farming. Traditional stories from different cultures.	Making a floor book. Making models.	Using an art package. Using a word processor with a concept keyboard to sequence text. Keying in text for a display.	Making hand prints in different colours. Making a frieze.	Singing rhymes with emphasis on the rhythm.	Awareness of other cultures.
EXTENDING VOCABULARY	Awareness of how time is measured. Counting backwards from ten.	Learning names of animals. Looking at buds. Classifying foods. Comparing fruits. Work on floating and sinking. Investigating sources of sounds. Exploring the senses. Awareness that light comes from the Sun. Recording weather.	Reporting events and telling stories set in the recent past.	Contrast of urban and rural scenes. Discussing islands and oceans.	Making a zigzag book. Making a floor book.	Using a word processor to write, edit and present text. Using clip art or an art package. Use of graphing software. Creating a database. Using a cassette recorder.	Making a frieze. Drawing images agreed on through discussion. Making composite pictures from magazines.	Making up a counting song. Making rhythmic percussion music for a weather song.	Talking about 'first' experiences. Awareness of the Sun's importance for life.
INFORMATION HANDLING		Investigating the growth of seedlings through practical experiments. Investigating the sense of touch. Looking at mirrors and reflections.	Asking older people about their experiences.	Observing and describing a real location. Drawing a map of the school's location, with directions.	Making an alphabet book. Discussing the designs and uses of hats. Making sweets and biscuits. Making models from junk materials. Looking at the school building.	Using a word processor to write, edit and present text. Using a concept keyboard to sequence text. Using an art package with colours. Using a cassette recorder.	Making a collage. Making a frieze. Illustrating a zigzag book. Making portraits of themselves and other people.	Singing 'The Teddy Bears' Picnic'.	Talking about likes and dislikes. Awareness of self from looking in mirror.
EXPLAINING AND UNDERSTANDING	Describing objects in terms of shape and size.	Investigating the sense of touch. Describing how a natural process (burning) works. Investigating the sense of sound.		Drawing conclusions from pictures of a 'busy' scene in a particular type of place.	Learning and teaching a craft technique. Making a zigzag book. Planning a 'guided tour' of the school.	Using a word processor to write, edit and present text. Using an art package.	Learning and teaching an art technique. Making wax-resist patterns. Describing a picture in detail.	Describing recorded sounds in terms of their properties.	Children's feelings about school.
OPINION AND PERSUASION		Thinking about the uses and dangers of fire. Discussing litter in terms of the properties of materials. Comparing different pets and their needs.	Awareness of how persuasive techniques can affect people's opinions.	Discussing the effects of litter on the environment.	Making models from litter. Making animal masks. Seeing how advertisements 'work' and creating a 'product' design for a cereal box.	Using graphing or pictogram software to display data. Using an art package. Using a colour printer. Scanning images onto a page. Using simple authoring software.	Making a frieze. Making an anti-litter poster. Making pictures to advertise a product.		Awareness of diversity of opinions. Talking about prejudices. Talking about emotions.
REASONING AND SPECULATING	Using hoops to arrange sets. Looking at size, shape and weight of objects.	Identifying animals from visual characteristics. Making rational deductions and hypotheses. Sorting and classifying objects.	Discussing narratives in terms of causes and effects.	Looking at holiday brochures. Thinking about people who do particular jobs.	Looking at everyday gadgets. Designing and making wrapping paper. Looking at the clothing and tools for different jobs.	Using a branching database to make an animal classification key.	Drawing 'holiday photos'. Making a collage. Painting pictures. Using potato prints or splatter-painting.		Accepting differences between people. Making group decisions.

SPEAKING AND LISTENING